Who Moved the Bridge?

By

Darlene Hodge

© 2004 by Darlene Hodge. All rights reserved.

No part of this book may be reproduced, stored in a retrieval system, or transmitted by any means, electronic, mechanical, photocopying, recording, or otherwise, without written permission from the author.

This book is dedicated, with deep appreciation, to my sixth grade teacher, Philip Gruchy, who first inspired me to write.

And

To Bob, my long suffering, but understanding husband, who has encouraged me throughout these many, many years.

One of those Notes From the Author

These stories are not presented in any particular order. They are, basically, a little visit, a little chat, where one story brings to remembrance another. Maybe you'd like to sit back, possibly over a cup of coffee, a glass of iced tea, or just take a quiet time to chuckle. If they make you laugh, that's the whole point. Laughing is good.

Table of Contents

The Flight of the Tractor

"That little plane was circling the field again today," I warned Bob. "We'd better get some camouflage netting."

He did not believe, as the children and I professed, that the Smithsonian Institute was deeply interested in our haying equipment.

The rest of the family thought it was funny that each summer, while we were haying, a light plane would circle us for a while, and then fly off. Two or three days later, it would return and do a replay.

One of the children suggested that it might be a Soviet spy plane taking propaganda pictures about "The Obsolete American Farmer." Bob didn't think that was funny either. Our family enjoys haying; after it's over for the year. We each have our favorite jobs, and least favorite. I always get dibsies on the baler. I do pretty well since that first year when I ran over Bob's foot with the tractor. It was only his crippled foot. There really was no need for him to be so upset.

"After all," I had pointed out reasonably. "Be thankful it wasn't your good leg. Then what would you do?"

The only other incident, except the time that he had to jump and duck to keep from being decapitated by the baler chute when I turned too quickly, was the first time I hauled the hay home alone.

We make a little trail to the field each summer and replace a rickety, makeshift bridge with logs and brush. It's barely wide enough for the equipment to cross and it rattles and creaks something fierce. Just the thought of hauling the rack with one hundred twenty bales of hay over the thing causes palpitations.

"Can you handle it?" Bob asked. "Oh sure," I told him. "Don't worry. I know what to do."

"Don't go flying across the field, either. Probably you'd better just stay in low gear."

"Yes, Dear."

Low gear meant being passed by every elderly snail and turtle in the field. Twice. It was ridiculous. I shifted into second. That was a lot better. At least a body could tell that they were moving. Third gear was even nicer. A bit bouncy, but at least I would get the hay to the barn the same year as I started. I made a wide arc at the end of the field and headed down hill. The tractor began to pick up speed. I eased the brake pedal. Nothing happened. I stood up and pressed the pedal as hard as I could. If anything, it picked up speed. I didn't know that tractors could move so fast. The trees and bushes beside the field began to blur.

"Stop! Stop! Help! Help!"

There was no help available. I was alone, gasp, on a runaway tractor.

I hung on with all my strength as we raced downward. I turned and looked at the hay stacked high above. Surely, it was gaining on me. Then two bales flew off and landed ahead of the tractor. I swerved and watched in horror as the bales still in place, swayed off to the left. I closed my eyes.

"Jump!" I shouted to myself. Visions of John Wayne leaping from various wagons and horses rose in my mind. I tried to jump, but my hands wouldn't loosen their grip on the steering wheel.

I couldn't keep my seat either. I would bounce high in the air, then land back on the tractor seat with a thud. Then watch helplessly as my feet bounced above the steering wheel. It wasn't rhythmic, though. Just bounce, bounce, feet, or maybe, feet, feet, bounce.

Finally, the tractor began to slow as the hill leveled off to flat land, and everything got back into its proper place, seat on seat and feet on brakes.

I looked back toward the hayfield. Apparently, no one had noticed my plight. Good. Directly behind me though, eleven bales of hay dotted the landscape, telltale evidence of my misconduct. Ahead lay the bridge. Somehow, it didn't seem scary anymore. Then a shadow crossed in front. I looked up. The Russians again. They certainly got good propaganda footage that time. What title would they use for this, I wondered? "The American Farmer. Obsolete and Stupid." I winced. That was bad.

I waved to the plane. "Hey guys," I told them. "Us Americans, we might not all be too bright, … but we're tough and we learn."

I turned the tractor toward the bridge, in low gear.

In Defense of Dumb Animals

Flower almost got me killed.

Flower was a fifty-nine cent turtle that we had purchased from the little pet shop down the street and around the bend. He was cute and trained us well. We caught flies and fed them to him. Live. He would rush over to where we held his yummies, and claw excitedly at the side of the glass dish, which was his home. We dropped the food directly into his mouth. He ate raw hamburger and fresh worms, too.

"You know", I told Bob one day, "Flower needs an outdoor pond to swim around in and get more exercise. He needs more room."

Bob stared at me. "I suppose a little island to climb on would be necessary, too. Right?"

"Great idea", the kids and I agreed. We missed the sarcasm.

We all started digging the very next day and soon, a cunning little cement pond was prepared. It had a little island, though not too little, and a tree planted on the island. It looked awfully nice.

The neighbors thought we were a little on the daffy side to spend all that time and money on a pond for a turtle. I explained that the children could use it for their G.I. Joe battles and Barbie sunbathing. This did nothing to assuage their initial thoughts.

Flower loved it. The children loved it. The dog loved it. The cats weren't too impressed. Bob and I would sit on the porch swing and admire our handiwork, and congratulate ourselves on our fine humanitarian efforts toward one of God's lesser creatures.

Then one night it rained. Not like a gentle northern Minnesota rain. No, sir. This was a bucket pouring, plant crushing, street flooding, Texas rain. Lightening shredded the sky. Thunder crashes shrieked around the town, terrorizing and deafening the populace. I shivered under the covers and pillow, scrunched next to Bob, and wished for the day.

Bob snored away.

Then, I thought of the turtle.

"Bob", I cried, shaking him. "Flower!"

"Wha?"

"Flower is out in this horrible storm. He must be terrified."

Bob mumbled something about survival of the fittest, and went back to his snoring.

Something had to be done. Someone had to do what had to be done. There was nowhere else to turn. No one else who cared. I was the one. I scrambled out of bed and grabbed the umbrella. Out on the patio, sheets of rain pelted against my quivering body. I bent my head into the umbrella and advanced recklessly out into the yard.

Water was sloshing over the edges of the pond. I knelt down trying to find the little, terrified turtle.

"Flower!" I called.

Crash! A thunderbolt answered. The sky turned a dazzling white-blue. I waded into the pond. "Flower! Flower!"

Another flash of lightening, and another crash of thunder. Simultaneous light and sound.

I saw myself reflected in the bedroom window. There I stood in water past my ankles, wearing my pink baby doll pajamas, holding a metal tipped umbrella high above my head, and calling a turtle named Flower. All the while, the worst storm of the year flashed and crashed around the house and pond.

I wondered about the neighbors. Wondered if they were asleep. Wondered if they were, even now, calling one another on the phone.

"Look! Look out in Hodge's back yard. You're not going to believe this."

I envisioned newspaper headlines. Strange Tragedy by Lightening. The TV cameras panning over my remains. People glued to their sets at news time, shaking their heads in wonder as they stared. Would the TV people modestly cover my body before filming? I could hear my children explaining it all during Show and Tell at school.

I went inside.

Flower was gone the next morning when we went out into the rain drenched yard. We found him three days later, while we were weeding the rose bushes. He was having a grand time scrambling around, scarfing down grubs. He, apparently, had no remorse what-so-ever about my near demise on his behalf.

That didn't bother me at all, though; I mean, after all, he's just one of God's dumb creatures.

On a Roll

"You wanna go for a ride on the snowmobile?" Bob asked.

"Sure," I said, "why not?"

There was a lot of snow on the ground that year, and it seemed senseless not to put it to good use. The day was clear, not too cold, and we actually had some free time. We donned our gear, waved goodbye to the children and rode off together into the sunset.

We turned at the corner, crossed the road and entered a huge field that belonged to one of our neighbors. We stayed, politely, on the snowmobile trail that he had made, and skimmed along at a fair clip.

The wind whipped our faces, burning our noses and cheeks, drying our lips and stinging our eyes. Our knees were numb from the wind chill and our insides joggled about, trying to remain in their appointed places.

"Isn't this fun?" Bob shouted above the din.

"Terrific," I shouted back, forgetting how much I had whined about the cold while doing chores.

Suddenly, the snowmobile stopped.

"Why'd you stop?" I asked Bob. "We aren't anywhere."

"I didn't stop. The machine did," he informed me as he leaned forward to lift the hood and inspect the motor.

"Uh, oh," he said.

"What, uh, oh?"

"The belt is broken."

"So?"

"So, no go." He smiled sweetly, "We'll have to walk home."

"In this cold? Forget it."

"Okay," he said, swinging off the machine, "stay here."

"All right," I mumbled, "we walk."

Bob turned and stepped onto the snow beside the trail and sank up to his chest.

"This is deep snow," he observed, with a great deal of perception.

"Let's go back on the trail," I suggested.

He looked back. That was a long way to walk. He glanced at the road. "It's only about three hundred feet from here to the road," he said, "come on."

Gamely, I jumped in beside him. The snow was up to my neck.

"Now what?" I asked, trying not to sound too sarcastic.

"Now we get on top of the snow and roll to the road," he said.

"Surely, you jest."

"I'm not jesting," he replied somewhat shortly. The fun was beginning to wan and the cold was exerting itself, apparently.

Bob began waving his arms about and, slowly he worked his way to the top of the snow. Then carefully, he stretched out on his side. I watched in utter astonishment as he began to roll away.

"You look ridiculous," I laughed. "I'm not going to do that."

I waved my arms and worked my way to the top of the snow. Then, I stood up, and sank again. At this rate, I would still be working my way out, come spring. I yielded.

Giggles began to tickle inside me as I rolled atop the snow. I tried to suppress them, but the whirling view; snow, sky, Bob, snow, was too much. I laughed. Then I laughed some more. I began laughing so hard I had to stop rolling.

"Bob," I called faintly, weak from laughter. "Bob, wait."

I could hear him laughing up ahead. He laughed again and again. There even seemed to be an echo.

I looked up to see how much farther it was to the road. That's when I saw the source of the echo.

Two of our neighbors had stopped to help, but they were of no value to us. One man was leaning back against his car, his arms folded across his stomach. He was laughing. He had his heels dug into the packed snow beside the road, trying hard not to slip and collapse. The other was in like position. Their mirth rang out across the field, bounced off the recently deceased snowmobile, and circled and mixed with ours.

"Don't laugh," I called out to them. I sat up for a better view and was instantly vised, with my arms and legs pointing skyward, while my, uh, bottom sank straight down.

"Help! Bob! Help!"

Bob rolled back and grabbed my arm, dragging me back to horizontal.

"Hee, hee, hee," he said. "Hee, hee, hee, hee."

Meanwhile, back on the road, "Hee, hee, hee, hee, ha, ha, ha."

"Ho, ho, ho," I added, as we crawled and struggled up to the cars.

One of the neighbors gave us a ride home. He laughed all the way there.

"I was never so embarrassed," I wailed as we told the children of our adventure.

"Yeah," they sympathized. "It's too bad we weren't there."

"What could you have done?" Bob wanted to know.

"We could have sold tickets."

Veneer is Only Skin Deep

Somewhere, I read that we are just two generations away from reverting to the Dark Ages. I would amend that to roughly twenty minutes.

I once considered myself extremely enlightened, well educated, and sophisticated; especially regarding the commonly feared and unloved members of the insect community. For many years I proclaimed the rights of these unjustly maligned creatures to the unenlightened and superstitious public, who knew no better than to fear and slaughter these jewels of nature, for no other reason except that, “they were there”.

“Don’t kill the spider, she eats flies and mosquitoes.”

To those who refused to respond correctly to this dictum, I would lower my sights to their primitive and superstitious level.

“Don’t kill the spider, you’ll make it rain.”

This last, was not necessarily a wiser statement, especially during droughts. The spider was usually dispatched immediately, as a sacrifice to whatever rain god happened to be watching.

"Snakes are our friends they eat mice."

I actually have a slight problem with this last. I mean, mice are so cute. If one happens to be in our house, and no one else is around, I capture it in a coffee can and liberate it outside. Yeah, yeah, I know there are snakes out there, but if I don't see them, they must not exist. It really doesn't matter about the snakes, anyway. We have cats. Sigh!

The degeneration of my intellectual sophistication descended on a fine, sunny, house hunting day. The real estate agent had parked her van in front of a brick house, with a screened-in porch that over looked flowering lilac bushes. She checked her info papers. Three bedrooms. Full basement. Privacy fence. Just what we wanted.

The screened-in front porch was packed with bag upon bag of very expensive dog food. Fifty pound bags, to be exact. Dog lovers. A good omen. The first room we entered also contained dog food. And, bag upon bag of cat food. And, varied boxes and bags and cans of other animal feed.

What normally, would have been the dining room, was filled with darkened cages stacked around the walls, and across the shaded windows. Little sounds emanated from the cages; scratching, scurrying sounds, unidentifiable sounds. A heavy oppressiveness permeated the air, seemed to seep into our pores, into our hair follicles. My fingernails tingled. I drew closer to my husband and the real estate agent. We crowded into the kitchen.

The kitchen windows were covered with dark material. More cages. Black light lamps radiated a muted, reddish blue glow into the cages; glass cages covered with screening. I noticed movement beside me, and very nearly crumbled into a dizzying swoon, as a large boa constrictor softly glided past my thigh. With adrenaline surging wildly into my veins, I leaped to one side, nearly knocking over another glassed in cage. I glanced though the screen top, and felt the old adrenaline pump kick into overdrive. Scorpions! At least a half dozen scurrying, black scorpions, with tails curved menacingly over their backs. I thought I heard clicking from another cage. I tried, almost successfully, not to hyperventilate.

"Did you want to see the basement?" The real-estate agent didn't sound too very enthusiastic.

"No! Uh, no. Not the basement."

As we climbed the stairs to the bedrooms on the second floor, I stayed away from walls. Touched nothing. Watched everything. By this time, it really didn't matter. At least seven senses were on high alert.

We finished the tour. Outside, at last, we climbed into the van and buckled into our seat belts. As we pulled away from the curb and into the light suburban traffic, I reached for the paper on the dash, to read about the next house on our list. Surprisingly, my hands were not shaking, though I could still feel the adrenaline roaring around looking for release. It got it. From the underside of the white paper in my hand, long thin, dull-brown legs curled their way over the edge. More legs swarmed, waving and dragging their elongated brown, spider-body, over the top.

There is no recall of how it happened, but I was suddenly unbuckled, out of the van, and standing on the sidewalk screaming, “Kill it! Kill it!”

“It’s just a little granddaddy-long-legs spider,” Bob tried vainly to assure. “It’s not going to hurt you.”

I didn’t care. Survival of the fittest was raging through my whole being. Reverting me to a more simple, primeval life and understanding.

“Kill it! Kill it!” I screeched, “we need the rain!”

The Fire Truck

Everyone is important. Wherever we may be, whatever situation we may encounter, we can make a difference in the lives of others. This philosophy has always encouraged me in all my varied endeavors.

"Let's go! Let's go! This is timed," our chief yelled, as he waved us off toward the specified site to pump water from the lake into our huge fire truck.

We were on a training exercise with two other rural volunteer fire departments, and we didn't want to look unprofessional. Even though that's exactly what we all really were.

Bob, my husband of over forty years, and I leaped, … okay, okay, we climbed, into the truck and roared off into the sunset. Actually, we eased out of the parking lot at a less than speedy pace because I had never driven this particular truck before. We headed slowly down a narrow winding road.

In a short amount of time, however, I had gotten the hang of driving the rig and soon we were bouncing along the gravel road, watching for the sign that would point us to the water fill area.

"B-B-B-Bob," I shouted, "w-w-w-why iisss iitt sssoooo bbbouncyyyy?"

We stopped the truck and maneuvered the seat a great deal closer to the steering wheel, and gas pedal, and brakes. Being five foot three has its disadvantages when driving a fire truck. It was still bouncy but at least I was able to give myself ballast, so to speak.

"There's the cut off," Bob yelled.

"Where? Where?"

"You just passed it. No sign."

I stopped the truck. We had just driven down a perpendicular hill and the turn was not at a ninety degree angle. It was more like a two-hundred-ninety-nine degree angle. I would have to back up. On the narrow gravel road. Up a perpendicular hill. I am not very proficient backing up any size vehicle under ideal circumstances. I was not happy. My mother-in-law's son was not happy.

"Look out!" "Go left!" "Go right!" "Go forward!" "Go backward!" "Go sideways!" Bob swears that he did not give me those confusing directions, but I know that's what I heard. Eventually, we achieved success and finally found our way to the pretty little lake where another department's truck was having water pumped into its innards by a little floating portable pump. They capped it off and suddenly, the truck was lumbering on its way. It was reminiscent of those racing pit stops. For pregnant turtles. It was still very impressive.

"Okay," Bob told me, "back down to the edge of the lake."

"Back down this hill? It's not a hill. It's a ski jump. Do you see that man from the other department standing in the way? What if I miscalculate? What if the brakes fail? I could run over him? I don't even know the man. What if we wind up in the lake? Who will pull this great big humongous truck out? What will the chief say?"

"The chief is already here, watching you. The brakes won't fail. Would you like me to introduce you to the man from the other department, so that you will feel better if you miscalculate and run over him?" Bob does sarcasm well. "Just back it up," he growled, er, said.

With much ado, I got the truck into reverse. Ding! Ding! The safety bells chimed. I started easing down the ski jump toward the lake. I was over too far. I pulled forward. Backed up. Ding! Ding! Forward again. Then down. And down. At last I stopped, set the brake and leaped. Yes I did too, leap, because, of course, my legs won't reach the ground from the truck. It was built for long legged giants. As I say. I leaped to the ground and did all of the assorted stuff that you gotta do when you are doing this kind of assorted stuff. Soon, just like a waterlogged race turtle, we were off. We drove back up the ski jump, up the perpendicular hill, on to the parking lot, discharged all that water and someone else sped off for their turn at practice. They did stop for a few seconds at the edge of the parking lot. I must have forgotten to set the driver's seat back. We did ourselves proud, more or less. The rest of the crew had to work especially hard to make up for my abominable run time, and surprised even themselves at how efficiently they could handle the situation when the pride of the department was at stake.

Bob and I were just climbing into our car to head back to the fire hall when the chief called out to us.

"Hey, Bob! How about you meeting us at the hall and we'll let Darlene here, drive the truck back?"

"Me? Down that busy highway with all kinds of traffic? Why me? I'm not familiar with this truck."

"I know," he said, "I saw your attempts to maneuver down at the lake. That was the worst display of driving and backing that I have ever seen. You definitely need practice driving this truck."

"What about me?" Mike, one of our guys, wanted to know. "I drove the truck here. How do I get back to the hall?"

The chief pointed to the truck. "You ride shotgun," he said.

As I gingerly drove the truck out of the parking lot, I noticed several of my colleagues watching us leave. One removed his hat, and held it reverently over his heart, as the others somberly waved to us. Mike leaned far out of the window. He placed his hands together beseechingly. "Pray for me," he cried.

I felt so good about the whole training session. Why in just a few hours time I had, all alone, challenged our department to achieve goals much higher than they had ever imagined. And, most importantly, inspired the men to a deeper spirituality. I was proud.

Cruising Down the Beaver Darn

"We're going down to the darn in the river," I told our neighbor on the phone.

I was answering her question about time. As in, time to yak on the phone for a while.

"The darn?"

"Yes. The beaver darn. We want to see how it's doing since last year."

"Are you walking?"

"Nope. Thought we'd take out the old canoe. I kinda hinted around to Bob that we haven't been canoeing much lately."

"And he caught on to your hinting?" My neighbor was flabbergasted.

"Of course. He's not totally dense, you know."

What I didn't tell her, is just how very fine a line separates dense, and totally dense.

The conversation containing the "hint" went something like this:

"Honey," this is Bob now. "Honey, the folks down the road asked to borrow our canoe next week. Their boy is coming home from college and they want to go camping for a few days. I told them okay. Okay?"

"Sure," this is me, talking sweetly. "Sure, they might as well. Why not just let them keep it at their house all year round? After all, they are the only ones who have used OUR canoe in the past several years. Decades maybe. We never go anywhere in it. I mean, just because we live a quarter mile from a river means nothing. They might as well use it. If the poor canoe depended on us to use it, it would be old and turned back to dust, or whatever canoes come from. I'm certainly glad SOMEBODY gets to use it."

"Honey," Bob again, "Would you like to go canoeing tomorrow?"

The next day we tied the canoe to the top of the car and set off for the river. Our canoe is not your ordinary run-of-the-mill canoe. Oh, no. Bob picked it out many years ago when all of our children were at home. He bought the world's largest canoe. It's not an easy piece of equipment to move.

We wrestled it into the water and climbed aboard.

Seated in our respective places, we began our journey to the beaver encampment. We went around tight bends. We went past rocks and fallen trees. We scraped across a submerged rock.

"What are you doing?" Bob called out sternly, from the back of the canoe. "Didn't you see those little ripples that warn you of submerged objects?"

"I wasn't looking at the water. I was trying to keep from being decapitated by those tree branches that you were driving us into, with no regard to our safety," I replied in a soft ladylike voice.

"Well, keep your eyes open."

We paddled on. The quiet beauty of the riverbank, the soft ripple of the water as we slowly traveled along, somehow hushed all thoughts of that other world of harsh reality. We had left noise, and care, and worry, and fear, far behind us. It was as though we were enveloped in our own peaceful sanctuary.

"Bob," I screeched, er, softly. "Left! Left! You're running us into the bank!"

Too late. We scrunched over a log and up into the muddy riverbank. A tangle of tree branches and weeds and bushes all forgot their vows of never moving from their positions of stability when humans are present. In all the excitement, they leaped from their rooted places and attacked us mercilessly.

"Can you push us off of here?" Bob snarled.

"I can't," I replied gently while glowering toward the sky.

Long silence from behind me, as I struggled with the branches, and the weeds, and the trees, and the thorns.

"Darlene, where is your paddle?"

"It's caught up here in the tree branches above my head, and I can't get it untangled."

"How did you get it in a tree?" Bob was shouting again.

"Well, you wouldn't turn left, so I was switching sides and, anyway, it's not my fault. You were supposed to be guiding. Hah!"

Bob is man enough not to back away from admitting his mistakes. He just pushed and pulled and rocked the canoe until he finally got us free. He retrieved my paddle and handed it forward to me.

"Thank you," I said politely. Then I saw them. Eight hundred thousand great big, ugly, ferocious, man-eating spiders were in my part of the canoe.

I began to pound them with the edge of the paddle. Pound, pound, crash, hammer, crush.

"You are going to punch holes in the bottom of the canoe," Bob, speaking very calmly now. Resigned.

"I don't care," I said through grinding teeth. "If we go under then the spiders will drown." Pound, pound, crash, hammer, crush.

Bob, even more calmly. "There are leeches in this river."

In this country, only the strong survive.

Nobody in Our Family is Perfect

"We have to go through the car wash," my dad informed the family.

We were visiting my parents in Texas, and they had taken us to Padre Island, on the Gulf Coast. I didn't see the reasoning for the need of a car wash. We were all tired and just wanted to go home.

"Salt," Bob told me. "Just sitting out in the open here and not even touching the water, cars rust. The air is salty."

I thought that was pretty strange, but kept my mouth shut for a change.

We drove up to the car wash. It was just a bunch of pipes and hoses, free-standing out there in the open. It got the job done, I guess. It looked well used.

Dad's station wagon was crammed full of people, dogs, fishing equipment and other necessities for a day at the beach. My eighty-year-old grandmother was seated in the place of honor. By the window, front seat.

Grandma was from the old country and her English wasn't always so good. If a conversation went too fast, she sometimes got left in the abyss of not knowing what in the world was going on.

"Everybody ready?" Dad called to us.

We were all too tired to be excited about anything more. We just dumbly nodded our heads.

Dad dropped the coins into the slot and carefully drove the car into place.

Suddenly, the car was bombarded on all sides with harsh streams of icy cold water.

We knew, first hand, that the water was icy cold. Grandma had failed to roll up her window.

Shrieks, screams, hollers, yells, barks, yelps.

Dad pulled the car out of the line of fire. Everyone slammed open their doors and jumped out to go save Grandma.

Grandma was sitting totally still. She was looking straight ahead. She was soaked. Just plain soaked.

We all grabbed towels and sweaters and tried to comfort her.

"Are you all right? Are you cold? Speak to us."

She turned to my dad. "Why did you do that?" she said.

He explained about the salt and rust, and all. She smiled.

"Okay," she told him, "I guess we should go through there again. Maybe I should pay this time."

Dad assured her that she didn't have to pay. He watched as she carefully rolled up her window.

The rest of us climbed back aboard and he drove around to the car wash entrance once again.

This time he looked all around the car. All windows were closed. Everyone was quiet.

"Everybody ready?" he called.

We all nodded.

Dad dropped the coins into the slot. He carefully drove the car into position.

Suddenly, the car was bombarded on all sides with harsh streams of icy cold water.

We knew, first hand, that the water was icy cold. One door had not been closed tight. The water pressure and the angle of the hose forced the water into the car, spraying everyone. Again.

Shrieks, screams, yells, hollers, barks, yelps.

Dad pulled the car out of the line of fire. Everyone jumped out. Just because that seemed the right move at the time. We were all laughing. Everyone but my dad. His sense of humor was, er, dampened.

We all piled back into the car. Dad personally checked all the doors. He checked all the windows. All closed.

"Everybody ready?"

We all nodded dumbly, suppressing giggles.

Dad dropped the coins into the slot. Carefully he drove the car into place.

Suddenly, the car was bombarded on all sides with icy cold water.

We knew, first hand, that the water was icy cold. Dad had forgotten to roll up his window after he dropped the coins into the slot.

Shrieks, screams, yells, hollers, barks, yelps.

Dad pulled the car out of the line of fire. We all slammed open the door and jumped out, laughing.

There was no reason to jump out, but we had no choice. It had become a tradition by now.

"Can we go through there again?" someone shouted. "Let's see what happens next."

"No," my dad growled in his very fiercest Air Force Sergeant voice.

"We're going home. Now. The car is washed enough."

It rained all the way home. We kept the windows shut.

The Truth About Horses

Some people think that I'm silly for being afraid of horses. Actually, I'm not really afraid of horses. I just respect the fact that they are very big and have very small brains. This means that they do not understand, that when they step on your foot and you are screaming and writhing in agony, that they are the reason. When you try to push them away, they like to lean closer to you. This is to ensure that all of the bones in your foot are shattered, rather than just simply broken.

The truth is, of course, that horses are extremely intelligent creatures, which makes them extremely dangerous, if they happen to have a diabolical bent, which they do. They like to pretend that they are misunderstood, and they make accusations against innocent people, too.

Chancy is our old mare. She has no problem when it comes to drinking water. She, of her own volition, stands out in the rain. All rain. She gallops through the field after a good rain, splashing through puddles.

All is well and normal. However, if she has a rider on her back and she sees a half-inch puddle of water within a three-mile radius of her hooves, she immediately goes into hysterics. This means that she begins shying and screaming and traveling in tighter and tighter circles. If she were wearing a skirt, she would, no doubt, lift it above her ankles and rush to jump on the nearest chair.

My personal opinion is that she does this to add an element of excitement to her life, and to the life of her rider.

Chancy's daughter, Minny Soda, is totally different. Nothing frightens her. No sir. She frightens others. Me, for instance. She does it purposely, too.

Bob says that isn't true. She just likes to be petted and loved. Hah! He wasn't home the day she terrorized me in the well house.

We had just moved out to the country and were still enamored with the old fashioned, pure, back to nature, life style that we had adapted.

We had gone to the well house to get a couple of buckets of water. Rebekah was just tiny and therefore unable to understand the precarious predicament that we were facing. We were chattering and laughing, little realizing the harrowing experience that was about to descend upon us.

I pumped water into the buckets. Rebekah had her little hands on the pump handle, helping. Then I turned. Gasp!

"Minny's out!" I cried.

"Where, where?" The innocent child shouted.

"Don't step outside or she'll trample you into the ground," I warned calmly, not wanting my little daughter to become needlessly frightened.

Rebekah poked her head out the door and shouted, "Hi, Minny!"

This was all the encouragement the malevolent, six-month-old equine needed. She galloped straight to the well house door.

Acting with quicksilver thinking, I grabbed the child and slammed the door, just as Minny sped up to us, momentarily quashing her plans of mayhem in the well house.

"Why did you slam the door on Minny?" Rebekah wanted to know.

She was much too young to burden with the cares of this world, so I just brushed the question aside.

"She wants to kill us," I said, casually.

The horse trotted around the building several times. She kept her eye on the door and moved in swiftly whenever I pushed it open a tiny space to see if it might be safe to dash to the house for our lives.

"I wanna pet Minny! I wanna pet Minny!" my daughter cried, obviously terrified beyond reason.

It would be several hours before the older children came home from school. I was on my own.

I tried to think.

That didn't work.

I peered fearfully out the door. The horse was nowhere in sight.

"Quick, child," I cried and grabbed her hand. I grabbed a bucket of water, too. We would need water if that fiendish creature decided to besiege the house.

We were out in the open now, away from any form of safety. We hurried. Suddenly the plunkity, plunkity sounds of the filly's hooves on the gravel driveway could be heard. I glanced back. It had been a trick.

She had seen us. Now she was bearing down on us, bent upon destruction. I dropped the pail of water, scooped up my helpless child, and beat the horse to the door by bare inches.

We were barricaded against her onslaught for a long, long time. She kept walking around the house and peering in the windows until the big kids got home from school.

Her diabolical plan to terrorize me, and discredit me, were totally fulfilled.

"Poor Minny," I heard our eldest son, Skip, say sympathetically, as he patted her neck and led her quietly back to the barnyard. "Did Mom scare you?"

We're Not Crying Over Spilled Milk

"What in the world are you doing?" my friend asked one hot summer day.

I glowered unkindly.

She cautiously walked over to the stove, and peered into the big vat that contained one arm. Mine. It was still attached to me, however. She smiled a big, toothy smile.

"I repeat," she said, "what in the world are you doing?"

"Would you believe me if I told you that I'm really a brain surgeon, and that I'm scrubbing for surgery?"

She shook her head.

"Would you believe me if I told you that we are really very poor, and this is the way I must flavor the soup for supper?"

Same response.

"How about a top secret war department experiment. This is part three?"

"No," she murmured.

"Actually, I'm stirring the curds for this batch of farmer's cheese that I'm making."

She looked into the vat again. "I don't think I believe that, either," she said.

Over the natural course of events, the one sweet dairy cow that we had purchased, turned into two dairy cows. We were the mass producers of lots and lots of milk.

We hadn't planned on having two cows, but when our newly acquired bovine began acting in a rather strange manner, some warning bell clicked in the far recesses of my mind. That book that I had borrowed from the library did say somc such about such situations.

I dialed the number of the fellow who was in charge of artificial insemination in our area. His wife answered the phone. I identified myself.

"Yes," she said. She knew who I was.

"Uh, er." What in the world was I supposed to say? None of the book's phrases came to mind.

"Are you there?" she said into the phone.

"Uh, yes. I'm here. Uh. The reason I'm calling is, is."

I could feel my face flushing a deep red. I had to say something.

"Well, you see," I said breathlessly, "Our cow wants to get married."

Later, I learned the proper terminology.

After the new calf arrived, the new mommy cow gave lots and lots of milk. We drank milk; I made butter, cottage cheese, farmer's cheese, cheese cake. We sold milk to friends. We gave milk to friends. We fed milk to the chickens. We bought a pig, and fed milk to the pig.

Every time I opened the refrigerator, gallons and gallons of milk would stare out at me.

"Somebody drink a quart of milk, quick" I would command.

"We are going to have to come up with some ideas about what to do with all of this milk, Robert," I told Bob, one especially milk abundant day. "There's just no more room in the refrigerator."

We couldn't sell it to a commercial dairy, government regulations being what they are, meaning ridiculous. We couldn't deliver the milk to anyone who wanted it, more of the same type of regulations. We couldn't just dump it out. Conscience this time.

"Some way will reveal itself," he assured me. "We'll figure out a way to get rid of it all."

We were sitting in the living room. Leah came in the back door. She was carrying in two more gallons of fresh milk. We heard the sounds of milk being strained. Sounds of milk being poured into bottles. Then we heard a slight squeal.

"Eeeeek!"

There was a humongous crash. Then, sounds of glass and plastic hitting the floor, crashing into each other. The horrifying sounds of thousands of gallons of milk, creamy white, thick, cohesive milk, sloshing onto the floor, splashing up the walls, thundering, rushing, spreading under the stove, the refrigerator, the cabinets.

Little sounds, too, of butter plopping onto the carnage on the floor, of eggs breaking. There was a small tinny sound, a small plate. Then utter silence.

Leah came to the living room door. Milk dripped from her hair, her clothes were drenched, her shoes were white and spattered with butter. She looked ready to cry.

Bob and I have been married a long time. We didn't even flinch. We looked at each other.

"Well," we said at the same time, "there's room in the refrigerator now."

Nothing to Fear But the Judge

Through a series of mixed-up communications, computer error, and human misunderstanding, I was driving around the countryside with no auto insurance. This is frowned upon by the state of Minnesota.

I became aware of this unhappy situation when I contacted my insurance agent to report a fender bender. He was as surprised as I to discover that the insurance had been cancelled some months before.

"Just explain to the judge," he said encouragingly. When he noticed my surprise, he added. "Of course, you'll have to go to court."

On the morning of the scheduled court appearance, I rounded up the confusing papers and canceled checks, waved off Bob's offer to accompany me, and stepped out in confidence. After all, I hadn't committed an intentional crime. A ten-dollar fine, or maybe just a fatherly scolding, was probably the worst that could happen.

"We'll send you a cake with a file!" one of the children shouted as I walked confidently to the car.

"Ha, ha!"

The courtroom was packed. It didn't look anything like the courtroom scenes on TV, or in the movies. I sat far to the back and looked, with some interest, at my fellow lawbreakers.

At last the judge came into the room. Suddenly court was in session. The fatherly figure that I had envisioned faded right away. He was, apparently not in the best of moods and didn't resemble Robert Young one bit.

I watched with mounting concern, as case after case was brought forward.

"How do you plead?"

"Guilty, Your Honor."

"Five hundred dollars or thirty days in jail."

and

"Two hundred dollars and ninety days in jail."

and

"Three hundred dollars and fifteen days in jail."

My heart began thumping heavily. The thought, "hanging judge," whipped through my mind several times. Gulp!

No one ever came back to their seat in the courtroom after he got through with them, I noticed. They all went out, one by one, through a side door near the front of the room, apparently never to return. They were always accompanied by a policeman. I wondered if they were allowed to say goodbye to family and friends.

The room seemed very warm.

The bailiff's voice dropped four octaves as he intoned, "The State of Minnesota against Darlene Wanda Hodge."

Feeling as though I had been accused of a mass murder, I walked slowly to stand in front of the room. When I got there, I noticed a curious clicking noise. I looked around. I couldn't place it.

The accusation was read aloud and the judge asked, "How do you plead?"

That's when I discovered what was making that loud clicking noise.

It was my teeth. They were clacking together so fast, I had to put my hand on my jaw to steady it enough to answer.

"Guilty," clatter, clatter, "Your Honor. B-b-b-b-ut I'd l-l-l-ike to explain-n-n-n." Clatter, clatter, click, click.

He gave permission for an explanation and I briefly described the situation. To prove my point, I reached into my pocket and pulled out the canceled check. I had planned to calmly hand him the check while I, with perfect tone and enunciation, explained to him just what had transpired with the insurance company.

Instead, I was shaking so badly, all that could be seen of the check was a blue blur fluttering up and down at the end of my uncontrollable arm. I shoved the check back into my pocket before it tore into shreds.

The judge sat there quietly. He shaded his eyes with his left hand and looked down at his papers.

The clicking noise was now joined by the thud, thud of my knees knocking together.

Finally, he looked up. "Darlene Wanda Hodge," he said. "I find you guilty as charged."

He wrote a big red "G" by my name, "…and fine you fifty dollars…"

Oh no. I thought, fifty dollars! He IS a hanging judge.

"…and suspend the sentence."

Suspend! Hanging! My hand flew to my throat.

"Come this way please," the policeman was saying to me. He guided me to the side door. The door no one ever came back through. It was over. I hesitated, then, head high, I bravely went out to meet my fate.

The door only led to the hallway. Bewildered, I looked around. "What now," I asked.

"Why you can go home now," the policeman said.

"Home? But the fifty dollars?"

"The judge suspended that. You don't have to pay."

"Oh, of course, that's what it means. I was a little flustered there for a minute."

Later, I assured the family, that all had gone, very nearly, as planned, with just a few inessential differences. "When you are an innocent person," I told them, "There is absolutely no need to fear."

(mis)Quotes From A Martial Arts Grandma

"Darn," (sort of), "the torpedoes!" "I have not yet begun to fight!" These famous words, spoken in moments of extreme provocation by some famous naval heroes, have been a great source of inspiration for many people. For me, too.

I like to think that I possess a fantastic ability to totally recall famous utterances by famous people during times of duress. But then, I like to think that I know something about karate, too.

Karate class has been a time of great duress for me; so I try very hard to recall famous utterances by famous people. Partly because I need all the inspiration I can gather just to keep me from collapsing, and partly because I cannot understand the utterances of our instructor.

"Mumble, mumble. Aiyk!"

The "aiyk" part is a signal for all and sundry to perform the move that he has ordered. The order being the mumble, mumble part. A quick glance at my younger classmates, who seem to understand him, reveals the position to me, and I then comply.

All of my classmates are younger than I am. Many are even younger than some of my grandchildren. There are a few oldies, however, meaning youngsters in their twenties.

This short, chubby, silver haired grandma, dressed in a white karate suit, looking, for all the world, like a gnome, causes much mirth in the ranks of observers outside the plate glass window of the gym. Just my being there, standing still, causes smiles.

"Stretching exercises," our instructor, Mr. de Sade, calls out. "Sit on the floor. Stretch your legs as far apart as you can. Now touch your forehead to your knee."

At first I thought he was joking, or that I had misunderstood, but no, they were all joining knee to forehead. I try. Unfortunately, over the years quite a bit seems to have come between my knee and my forehead.

"Next exercise. Legs still apart. Touch your chest to the floor."

I bend forward. Yep, there's the floor alright.

On the other side of the window, people are holding their shaking sides. They are dabbing openly at their eyes.

"Now quickly, lying on your back. Knees bent. Hands under your shoulders. Push up."

He demonstrates by lithely doing upside-down push-ups. All the other students are being lithe and all that.

I lay on my back. I am immobile. It is very humiliating.

Suddenly everyone is jumping to their feet. The instructor mumble shouts something and they all stand in a straight, intimidating stance. I scramble up and, creaking and panting, stand in a straight, intimidating stance, too.

Now we begin the hard stuff. The real karate, mumble, mumble. Aiyk! Stuff.

At first, I did try to read our instructor's lips, but I'm not sure he has lips. He does have a big bushy mustache in the general vicinity of lips. It doesn't help me, though. I don't read mustache, either.

"Dachshund breeding stance. Aiyk!"

Surely, that's not what he's saying. I blush anyway, and bend the old knees to assume an incredibly awkward posture.

"Fighting stance. Aiyk!"

My right foot slides back and points to the side wall. My left foot points straight ahead. My knees are bent. I take special care to keep my fists around the vicinity of my chins.

This is most important. Vital even. He who does not keep his fists near his chin must do push-ups.

"Thrust kick. Side kick. Round kick. Mumble kick. Half kick. Aiyk! Aiyk! Aiyk!"

"Maybe I should quit," I puff under my breath. "I'll never make it. I can't do it. It's too hard. I'm too old."

My joints creak with each kick. My bones ache. My next jump. Jump? That was a jump? Causes my muscles to cringe.

I open my mouth to announce my retirement from the class.

"No," I decide. I must continue. "I shall fight in the gym. I shall fight in the streets. I shall fight in the country side." Sir Winston would," never, ever give up." Neither shall I.

Somehow, over the months I persevere. I am paired with a tall, young, lifeguard type, man. We practice not quite hitting each other. The brown belts are helping us. Encouraging us.

I turn, twist my feet around, and give a strong backward kick, called, for some unknown reason, a sidekick.

Suddenly the world is a rainbow of beauty. I have accidentally connected. The young man stumbles backward. Holding his belly. "Aagghh!" he says.

The brown belts are in awe, their jaws drop down to their chests. They can't believe it. I can't believe it. I have kicked high and hard and executed a beautiful, perfect sidekick.

"I'm so sorry," I laugh seriously.

"It's okay," the tall, young, lifeguard type, man sighs bravely.

I have done it. I have finally experienced the ultimate satisfaction in life. Not only did I do something right, I did it in front of several credible witnesses.

Now I know that my physical abilities are just as sharp as my enormously impressive historical recall abilities. I am proud.

I think I'll go on in karate. Maybe I'll even get a black belt. After all, as Harry Truman must have said at some time in his life, "If you've got an objective to go for, then by golly, go for it all the way." Only

President Truman probably would not have said “by golly.”

So, I’ll just do what Teddy Roosevelt said, “talk softly and harbor a big kick.” Or something.

Bringing Home the Gold

"Well girls," I said menacingly, "I'm getting tired. Either work…" I paused to make sure they were paying attention, they were. Each had her head tilted to one side, the better to see me. "It's work or curtains for you. You'd better take heed."

I closed the door and stalked back to the house in disgust. Raising chickens was not all feather and eggs.

The books and pamphlets had all been pretty exciting. Everyone in the family was enthused by the time our first batch of day-old chicks arrived at the house.

Bob had made a snug, warm box with a light and thermometer. The feed and water awaited, and with much ado and fanfare, we placed each fluffy chick into its new home. Twenty-five chicks to be exact.

By morning there were twenty-four. I cried as I carried the poor, dead little critter to the swamp for burial. Two days later the survivors numbered twenty-one. I cried as I carried the little feathered carcasses to the swamp for burial.

Day four. Eighteen live chicks. I was exasperated as I stomped toward the swamp.

I called a friend.

"Help," I wailed, "my chicks are dying all over the place. What am I doing wrong?"

We went over the list. Feed. Water. Heat. Draft. Light. Gravel.

"No gravel," I told her, "I use newspaper instead."

"Newpaper? For what?"

"For to keep the bottom of the box clean," I explained knowledgeably.

As it turned out, the gravel was not for sanitation, as in kitty litter, but for aid to their little digestive tracts. I was mercilessly starving them to death. Somehow, I had missed that rather important tidbit of information in the pamphlets.

Eventually all was set aright. "Isn't this great?" I told Bob one evening. "Soon we'll have our very own eggs and fryers; and just think of the taste and the nutrients and the savings."

"Oh yes," he said, "about the savings. I just happen to have, in my possession, a cost list."

He drew a long sheet of paper forward.

"Look carefully, now. Here's the original cost of the twenty-five chicks, of which we now have fifteen left, you understand."

I nodded.

"The cost for that holding box for them. The feed. The, ahem, gravel, the thermometer. The cost of the chicken coop. The fencing around the chicken yard. The wiring for lights for them…"

"Stop!" I cried. "You can't count all of that up now. Wait for a few years. These chickens will have babies, etc., and then you'll see how much it's worth. In food, and enjoyment, and stuff like that."

The following spring brought more chicks. This time, a good old mamma hen took care of them and didn't loose a single one. This caused some comments in the household about abilities, but I ignored them.

Out of that batch, however, was hatched, the meanest, most cantankerous, malevolent rooster that ever lived. We couldn't keep him in the chicken yard. He had an uncanny knack for escaping. He attacked everybody that moved outside the house: the horses, the dogs, the cats, people. He even attacked the geese. The little children became afraid to walk out the door.

His final hour on earth came when he zeroed in on our youngest child, talons at eye level. I grabbed her and ran, he chased us into the house, and I came out with an equalizer.

"This is fun?" Bob asked that evening as we tried to salvage some edible parts from the late, but not lamented, rooster.

"Not yet," I told him grimly, "but soon."

"I've been checking," he said, "so far we haven't saved any money on eggs or meat."

"Soon," I repeated. "Soon the savings, in eggs alone, will be apparent."

"That's good because, as of now, each egg that we get is worth, roughly, thirty dollars."

"Gulp," I gulped aloud. "Don't worry, Honey. Soon we'll be saving money. You'll see."

Winter. No eggs at all.

"Come on girls," I would cajole, "be nice and let's have some eggs."

Nothing. Nothing for a long, long time. Lots of food. Nice warm water. Lights, straw, shelter, but no eggs.

One night in desperation, I told them the story of the miller's daughter.

"The king told her to spin the straw into gold, or off with her head." They just sat there sullenly.

"Get the connection?" I asked. No response.

"We'll have some eggs by morning." I told Bob of my pep talk.

"You think that'll do it, do you?"

"Yep! I explained all about how valuable each egg is, as I left I told them, 'This is your last chance. By morning either lay some eggs or turn this straw into gold'."

So they did.

Dog Gone

Socrates was a beautiful, white, part St. Bernard. He was a loveable lap dog, whose idea of a hard day at the office was to roll, with slow dignity, from napping on his right side to napping on his left side.

"Is he of any use?" people would ask, while peering around his limp body, trying to find the person quashed down into the recliner chair, underneath him.

"Oh yes," would come the muffled reply. "He's a magnificent guard dog. We call him 'Brave Socrates'."

We had a guide rope that led from the clothesline, through the woods to the barnyard. It had been set up for our blind daughter, to aid her in accomplishing her share of the family's farm chores. The rope was useful to the rest of us, however, if we happened to be going out to the barnyard at night.

One dark night I happened to be going out to the barnyard. Bob and the boys were still working on the goat pen and I decided that they could probably use a little advice from me.

"Come on, Socrates," I called.

The girls stood in the doorway, listening to our progress as we made our way to the rope. Then, with one hand on the rope and the other holding Socrates' collar, I shuffled uncertainly down the winding trail. The night was so black that I could not even see the dog next to me. Through the trees, the light from the chicken coop was muted, and seem to make the pathway even darker.

"Well, Socrates," I said to quiet his fears, "it sure is dark."

He pressed closer to me.

We were relatively new to the area, and still had not an accurate account of all the giant grizzlies and man-eating tigers that lived on our forty. We had seen weasels and mink, had heard the owls at night, and had experienced the hair-raising shock of watching a huge fisher cat flash through the treetops. He easily wiped out the squirrel population, meanwhile sending the horses into a frenzy of terror. There was no guarantee that some fearsome denizen of the forest would not leap out and devour us before we reached the safety of the light. I laughed nervously, and sang, and even whistled a few bars.

"Good boy," I encouraged, "you are a brave doggy."

Our son, R.V. (no that's not a misprint), heard all of this commotion and decided that he wanted into the game. Carefully, he crept along the side of the chicken coop and melted into the darkness of the forest. It was simple to keep track of our progress. We were making a horrendous amount of noise.

"We're almost there, Socrates," I said, relaxing a little. "just a few more steps and we'll be safe and sound."

"Roooaaaarrrr!" R.V. bellowed out of the darkness.

I'm not absolutely certain if I climbed a tree and fell down, or if I just ran into two or three trees while traveling in a vigorous circle. However, I soon discerned the sound of my son's laughter, from my own pitiful screams and more or less calmed down.

"Where's Socrates?" I asked at last.

We searched the area with flashlights. We whistled and called. The dog was gone.

"Mom," Leah called from the house, "Socrates is here."

The dog had managed to get back to the house and cower behind the girls, before I had even managed to stop screaming.

"He sure is brave," Bob commented later.

"Well Dad," R.V. explained, "he has one stronger quality, I guess."

"What's that?"

"Survival of the fittest."

Selling Jewelry

"All normal women love jewelry," the man assured me.

I just nodded. After a statement like that, there was no way I would admit to him that my wedding band and a wristwatch were all the jewelry that I really bothered with, of my own volition.

"You will have no trouble selling our line of exquisite fashion jewelry. You'll see. Women will be calling you to book shows." He noticed my bewildered look. "We don't hold parties," he added loftily, "we hold fashion shows."

"Oh."

At the training meetings that followed the interview, I smiled my best smile, and tried not to look as nervous and out of place as I felt.

All the other consultants oohed and ahhed over the various pieces of jewelry displayed. They tried on earrings, and bracelets, and rings, and pins, with total enjoyment, bordering on ecstasy. I began to worry about my mental wellbeing.

"Which do you think is best?" my boss wanted to know.

"They're all very pretty," I hedged.

He patted my hand. "Speechless, huh?" he said. "The idea of having all of this beautiful jewelry at your disposal is just too overwhelming."

I couldn't think of anything to say.

"I'm selling jewelry now," I mentioned to my friends. I figured if they wanted to know more they'd ask. Nobody did.

I tried the door-to-door approach.

Knock, knock.

"Yes?"

"You don't want to have a jewelry party do you?"

I tried with more finesse.

Knock, knock.

"Yes?"

"This beautiful pin can be yours free, if you will only please, please, book a fashion show with me."

I got one booking and sold almost ten dollars worth of jewelry.

I decided to please everyone and try to sell make-up instead.

"Make-up is for to, 'make-up' for when nature forgot to give you beauty," I explained to one group of cold, humorless women.

They didn't think that was so amusing.

I booked another party elsewhere.

I carefully placed my kit on the table. Told no jokes, but went right to the meat of the matter.

"As we grow older," I said, hitting the right stride for attention getters. (I was twenty-six at the time). "Our skin begins to tattle on us. The whole world can see at a glance, just how old we really are." Now I had them!

I began pulling out cleansing creams and smoothing creams and night creams. And then the coup d'grace. With a flourish, I held up a very impressive jar.

"This," I said dramatically, "is the new vitamin E cream."

"Aha!" a lady shouted. "That's not true! Vitamin E doesn't do one thing for your skin. I've been waiting for you to bring that out. It's nothing but a big lie! I read all about it in a magazine expose`."

"But I didn't say anything yet."

"It doesn't matter. It's all a lie."

Somberly I put the vitamin E cream back into the kit. I took the next item.

"This is our new foundation make-up." I waited, no one interrupted. "We just shake it up, open the lid, press the atomizer, and poof, out comes just the right amount. Believe it or not, the foundation grows right on your hand when it hits the air, making it light and silky on your face."

I shook the bottle, opened the lid, pressed the atomizer button and a light chocolate blob appeared on my hand. It began to grow. More and more of the make-up oozed out of the bottle. Panic!

"Stop!" I yelled and shook the bottle to let it know I meant business.

More make-up. It started sliding down my hand, dropping quiet little puddles on the table and floor.

"No," I moaned. "Go back. Go back."

Squeaky little sounds came from my audience. Oooooh's, and aaaah's, and oh dear's, and such. The make-up kept materializing. I rammed the mutinous bottle back into the kit and closed the lid.

Everyone was still, except the lady of the house, who was busy mopping up.

"Well," I said, looking around for a towel and finally, in desperation, wiping my hand on my skirt. "Well," I said again. I looked at the lady of the vitamin E episode. A completely compassionless face. I looked around the room; they were all of the same mold.

"Well," I said heartily as I picked up my kit, "goodbye."

"I don't think there's too much out there for me to do to bring home the bacon," I told Bob later, after turning in my sales kit.

"That's okay, Honey," He said magnanimously.

"Is it all right if I just be here and cook and keep the house for you?"

"That's fine."

"How about if I just be here and cook?"

"That's okay, too."

"How about if I just be here?"

He didn't say anything. He just kissed me.

Language Barrier

My grandparents loved me dearly. They were from the old country and taught me useful little sayings in Serbian. I could say The Lord's Prayer, and tell folks that I was a, "good golden girl," and remind the cat to wash her ears. My own ears were attuned to "the sound of Serbian."

As I grew up, I often impressed my friends with my bilingual abilities. "Dobra," I would announce after taking a lick of an ice cream cone. "Blavo is my favorite color," I would gravely intone, when admiring a dress.

Bob was really impressed when we met. Especially since he had never heard of Serbia and was quite certain that we were all mispronouncing Siberia.

A few years ago, we decided to take a conversational Serbian class in Hibbing, taught by Father Kaseric. Thereafter, once a week, for twelve weeks, if I remember correctly, Bob and I drove into town to improve ourselves.

Now, Father Kaseric is a very brilliant man who probably speaks one thousand four hundred and fifteen languages, give or take one or two. Unfortunately, this ability was of no value to him when it came to teaching me. After two classes, he mistakenly thought he understood our situation.

"Don't vorry, Darlene, it takes time to get used to the sound of a new language. It will come. Bob has been hearing Serbian all of his life and that's why it's so easy for him. Don't vorry."

I didn't have the heart to tell him the truth; besides it was pretty embarrassing. So I vorried.

Most of the other students were in Bob's ability range, and studied hard and did fairly well. There was one man, however, who apparently, had been around Serbian all of his life. He was very, very good. He was, also, I decided, teacher's pet. He was a member of the law enforcement community and was definitely the STAR PUPIL of our class.

At first, I looked upon him with envy.

"Mr. Star Pupil, please come to the blackboard and write this sentence in Serbian."

Then I began to regard him with suspicion.

"Mr. Star Pupil, please translate this next paragraph into English."

Nobody could be that good. He was probably a plant to make me feel inadequate. Any minute now, I expected him to translate, *Gone With the Wind* aloud.

The students basically maintained a nodding acquaintance with one another, and once in a while might see each other in a store or driving by in a car. We would acknowledge with a smile, a wave, or a "How are you."

About a month after the classes were finished, I happened to be at a benefit basketball game alone. I was surprised to see Mr. Star Pupil there as a referee. He seemed a bit surprised to see me there, too. Except, of course, he couldn't seem to quite figure out if he knew me. I could almost see his mind working: "Now is that some lady I ticketed, or is she one of the kid's teachers, or is she on a wanted poster?"

I personally don't like it when I can't place a name to a face; so to be polite, I decided to give him a hint. Not that he would know who I was anyway, but at least it would be my good deed for the evening.

Decorum was the rule for the day here. A Mae West approach of, "Hi, remember me? We took Serbian classes together," just would not do.

I waited 'til the half time and walked up to where he stood. He was talking to some other men, mostly neighbors of ours.

"Good evening," I told him in my very best Serbian.

He turned completely around and stared at me.

"Good evening," I said again. This time I smiled my friendliest smile.

His mouth dropped open and he just continued to stare.

"Good evening," I said once more.

He still didn't answer, and I flounced off, disgusted.

Later I told Bob that Mr. Star Pupil wasn't that great after all.

"Sure he could function in a classroom setting, but when it comes to the real thing, he doesn't know what to do. I'm much better than he is, because I can at least put what I know into practical use. Hah!"

"Are you sure that you said it with the proper accent?"

"Of course, I'm sure. Any ninny can say, 'good evening,' with the proper accent," I retorted irritably.

"Let me hear you."

Bob thinks he's so superior all the time; but I acquiesced.

"I said to him, 'dobra jena,' and I said it three times and he couldn't even answer me."

Bob had that same stunned look on his face that Mr. Star Pupil had.

"You didn't!" he finally gasped.

"How do you do it? How do you do it? It's no wonder you're always getting into trouble. You were supposed to say, 'dobra vece.'"

"Oh, yeah, that's right. Then, what did I say?"

Bob shook his head in disbelief and started laughing.

"What you said," he chortled, "What you said was, 'good woman'."

Take Me Out of the Ball Game

Our women's softball team had a perfect record. No wins. The youngest player on our team was twenty-six years old. The oldest was forty-seven. When we played the other teams, it was almost like the mothers against the daughters. We had to modify our motto a little bit. It went, basically, like this. "It matters not if you won or lost, but if you finished the game." Fortunately, we played for fun, and we had a season of good solid fun.

We brought joy to everyone. To ourselves, of course, and to each of the other teams, as they roundly tromped us on their way to not being in last place.

About midway in the season, we were scheduled to play the league champs, a team that struck terror into everyone's heart, except ours, of course. We enjoyed a challenge.

As usual, we had arrived early at the ballpark to get in some practice. We were just getting situated, when a man in a dark uniform came groping his way toward us.

"Is this the women's softball league?" he asked, stumbling forward.

We told him it was.

"Good," he said, "I'm the umpire. Somebody guide me to home plate. I just had my eyes dilated and can't see a thing."

This was too much. "How are you going to umpire this game if you can't see?"

"I don't need eyes," he declared. "I just calls 'um, like I hears 'um."

It took us a while to decide that he wasn't serious, but his sense of humor encouraged us to do our best.

He watched us practice for awhile and asked incredulously, "Have you ever won a game?"

"Not one," we assured him.

"I can understand that," he said.

By the time it was my turn to practice batting, he was shaking his head rather sadly.

After watching my performance, he asked if I had ever made it to first base.

"Only when I walk," I told him.

The champs arrived about this time, and it was pretty obvious that they knew who they were playing against. They were very relaxed, even jovial.

By the bottom of the fourth, our score was zero and the champs were somewhere in the astronomical numbers. Then Helen stepped up to the plate. Helen was our pitcher. She stood about four foot three and weighed about seventy-five pounds. She struck terror into no one.

On the second pitch, Helen swung, connected. The ball flew forward nearly two feet. We were all shocked. Helen most of all.

"I hit it!" she said. "I hit the ball!"

"Run Helen!" the coach shouted. "Run! Run!"

We all began screaming, "Run! Run!"

But Helen just stood there, a look of pure amazement on her face. "I hit the ball!"

The champ's pitcher raced forward to scoop the ball off the ground. She glanced at Helen.

"I hit the ball," Helen told her.

"Run!" the pitcher shouted at her, "run to first base."

"Hellen ran!" We were all screaming, "Run! Run!"

By this time the pitcher was sitting on the ground, her feet straight out in front of her. Laugh tears were streaming down her face and she barely had the strength to toss the ball to the first baseman, who was doubled over, holding her sides, laughing and coughing. She missed the ball as Helen rounded first and headed resolutely toward second base. Safe at second!

Everyone was screaming and laughing, except the umpire.

"Play ball!" he ordered.

By the time it was my turn at bat, we had two outs. Helen was on third and the bases were loaded.

"Tough position for you," the umpire greeted.

I nodded. "Oh well," I sighed, "somebody has to make the losing swing."

The pitcher sized me up. No problems foreseeable, and she pitched.

I let it go by. "Never swing at the first ball," our coach had warned us.

"Strike!" the umpire called.

I glanced accusingly at coach. He smiled.

Soon, too soon, I found myself in that dread place. The bases loaded. The count three and two.

The pitcher checked her base. I glanced nervously at coach. He was still smiling. I looked at the umpire and grinned. He glared past me. I'll go down swinging, I decided.

The pitch! The swing! I whirled totally around. The ball thudded into the catcher's mitt, behind me.

"Ball four!" The umpire cried. "Take your base!"

He glowered into the sea of astonished faces.

"Ball four?" I asked.

"Ball four," he said firmly.

"Way to go!" someone yelled. Applause and shouts from teammates and opponents alike.

I trotted obediently to first base, hands raised in triumph.

"Good game," the first baseman grinned at me.

"Our best yet," I assured her.

"The most fun we've ever had," she said.

We lost the game, of course. But we finished it.

A Kinder, Gentler Wife

Fuzziness covered my eyes. I blinked awake, sort of. Bob had swung the car across the road and was slowly driving up to face another car, parked on the shoulder. Apparently, the driver had flashed his lights to ask for help. The hood was open.

"What's going on?" I mumbled.

"Somebody's got problems," Bob said, as he opened his door.

It was bitterly cold on that hockey tournament night, that year. I glanced toward the back seat. Our children were asleep. I closed my eyes. Bob didn't need me out there. What could I do if someone's car didn't work? The only answer that I have about cars is; if it doesn't start when you turn the key on, then you're out of luck. You gotta buy another car.

I heard our hood release being pulled and opened my eyes slightly. The hood popped up and in the light of the headlights of the two cars, I could see several pairs of hands.

I sat up straight. There was something, definitely, wrong.

I slid back down into the seat to get a better view through the narrow opening between the body of the car and the now, wide open hood. I gasped, as a thrill of fear flashed through me. Bob was in grave danger.

There must have been five or six young men, right around twenty years old. They were out there, gathered around my poor, helpless, Iron Worker, husband. I couldn't see their faces, but I knew that they, no doubt, looked sinister.

Since my daughters had reached the ages of fifteen or sixteen, I had noticed that all the young men in that age group had begun to look sinister and, well, evil lately. Not like my own grown boys, who with their beards, and bushy black eyebrows and strong muscular arms, looked exactly what they were. Good, and kind, and gentle.

Wicked, sinister laughter could be heard now. Poor Bob. What would happen to him now? I did not need to ask. After they had beaten him to a pulp, and took the eleven dollars out of his wallet, then, then, they would turn to the innocent occupants of the car. My poor, helpless children.

I peered more carefully. I could not see faces. Just jackets, and hands, and blue jeans. Hands! Oh, no! One of them was wearing brass knuckles.

I had to save my husband and children. I was wide-awake now. I slipped into the driver's side. There was only one way out of this danger. It was not going to be easy.

"This is going to be messy," I said aloud.

I would put the car in gear. Then the first move that they made to attack Bob, I would ram them between the two cars, thereby breaking all of their legs. Then I would back away, drive off fast, and stop for help at the nearest house, which I knew to be several miles away, and call for help.

I realized that Bob's legs would be broken, too, but at least his life would be saved; and the children's. Besides, he already had one bad leg, so it shouldn't be too upsetting for him.

More sinister laughter. They were getting ready to attack. I slowly eased my foot onto the accelerator. I glanced out there again. Bob was reaching for his wallet. He was handing them a card. He was shaking hands with the fellow in the brass knuckles.

"What was going on out there?" I demanded when Bob climbed back into the car.

"Their gas line froze up. When we get home, I'm going to call a friend of their's in town, to bring out a can of Heet for them. It'll be quicker to call from our house, than to go all the way back into town and then back here."

He glanced at me. "Don't worry about them. They'll be warm enough. They're from out of town. The hockey tournament and all. They were prepared for the cold. I gave them my card in case they needed more help."

I mulled this around in my mind for awhile.

"Didn't it hurt shaking hands with the guy with the brass knuckles?"

"Brass knuckles?"

"Yeah. That sinister looking guy, whose face I couldn't see, was wearing brass knuckles."

"Sinister? Honey, I don't think you were fully wake. They were just a bunch of kids off to see the game. Nobody looked sinister, and the brass knuckles that you thought you saw were just gloves with holes on the tops. They're driving gloves. I imagine that they're the fad now, or something."

"Oh."

We drove along a few more minutes.

"I thought that you were in grave danger, and I was going to save you."

He laughed. "Honey, if I had been in danger out there, there was no way that you could have helped."

"I might have thought of some way."

He patted my hand. "Thank you for worrying about me, but really, what could you have done? You're too sweet and gentle to think up the kind of violence it would take to save me from five guys with brass knuckles."

"Yes, Dear," I said softly.

Mt. Crucial

We clung there on the side of the cliff. My friend, just above me, gasping for breath, looking for a higher handhold, a more secure footing.

My left hand was wrapped around an exposed tree root. My right hand sought, and found, a slight outcropping of rock. I gripped firmly. Then:

"AAAAggghhhh!"

"What? What?" my friend cried.

"My hand! You're standing on my hand!"

She had found a more secure footing.

"Why aren't you up here, instead of me?" she snarled. "It was your bright idea to climb this mountain, anyway."

"Yeah! Well I didn't hear any protests from you." I countered with all the sarcasm that I could muster. We were best friends. Teenagers.

"Besides, this isn't a mountain. There are no real mountains in Newfoundland. You wanna see real mountains? Go to Colorado."

"You think the States are so great? Go back to the States, Yankee!"

"Newfie!"

We continued our climb. Still best friends.

I tried to pull myself up another few inches. Something tugged at my blouse. It was hooked on a sharp rock. I pulled harder.

"I tore my blouse," I said proudly.

"You should see my blouse."

"It's worth it, though. I'll bet we're the first people ever to climb this…er…mountain," I finished sheepishly.

"Mt. Crucial," my friend offered. "It may not be a real mountain, but it's at least a mt."

That sounded reasonable.

At last, we reached the summit. I felt so proud. If only I had brought an American flag. I could have planted that flag and stood there saluting, or whatever one does when one plants a flag on a mt. top.

I looked at my friend. She, too, had a look of pride and accomplishment on her face. It's a good thing that I didn't bring an American flag, I thought. We might have started World War III.

"We did it! Hooray! The very first human beings to climb up here."

Then we saw the big rock. Over on the other edge. A huge rock covered with initials and names, painted, or carved, or lipsticked. Apparently, we were not the first to conquer this mt., after all. We hadn't done anything special.

We walked closer. Slowly. Defeated. There, on the other side of our Mt. Crucial, was a path. We could not believe it. A path. A simple, anybody-could-climb path. We felt so much better. We were vindicated. Gratified. Revitalized. After all, just about anybody could climb up on a path.

We sat there on the top of our mt., surveying the beautiful bay that lay before us. We were secure in the knowledge that we had done something special, something grand. We had met the enemy on his terms and we had won. A path! We sneered derisively.

Our descent was spectacular. Naturally, we disdained the well-worn path that transformed our mt. into nothing but a high hill. We went down the real side, slipping and sliding face forward, falling, jabbed by sharp branches and rocks. It was great. We were bruised and bleeding. Our clothes were very nearly shredded, our shoes destroyed.

We were conquerors. We were over comers. We were victorious over extreme odds. We were grounded for two weeks.

Ah, Country Living

The sudden sounds of dogs barking and horses screaming blasted me awake. Then, above it all, rang the thundering vocalized challenge of our German shepherd, Obediah. I sat up and scanned the woods outside our bedroom window. Obie was racing through the trees toward the barnyard, where the horses were still screaming hysterically, kicking and thrashing at the wood and metal door of the barn.

Most people, I would assume, faced with this type of situation, would no doubt haul out the old Smith and Wesson, and roar out into the night tackling any problems that presented itself.

Most brave people would. But me? Well, I am more inclined to using a great big military tank. One with huge turret guns that revolve slowly, intimidating any creature in its path. Unfortunately, we don't have one of those. I woke Bob.

"Honey," I hissed, "something's wrong with the horses."

"Urmmph," he said. He didn't even open his eyes.

What to do, what to do. We had company. City people, company. A whole house full of them, as a matter of fact. I didn't want to disturb them. We had all had a rough day sightseeing, fishing, and catching up on old times.

Bob was exhausted; besides, he had to go to work very early in the morning. He was, "walking iron," back then and definitely needed his rest.

It was all up to me. I would be brave and go into the dark and eerie night alone. Just me and my dog, and four or five rifles, pistols and maybe a machete or two, that should equalize up to whatever was out there terrorizing the animals.

I slipped on my shoes and started down the stairs. Obie met me half way. He was excited and turned around with a jump. He ran out the dog door and then back in. He ran to the kitchen door and began to paw at it. It was clear that he wanted me to follow him outside. I followed him, sans weapons.

The moon was so bright that each leaf and blade of grass seemed visible. I hurried to the barn, which now seemed ominously quiet.

I could see nothing untoward in the field. I turned back to the north side of the barn. No moonlight here. Just deep, dark, foreboding shadows. Slowly I eased along the pathway, thick woods on one side, the strong barn wall on the other. We really do need a little tank, I decided.

Suddenly, out of the gloomy darkness, a huge, dark, hulking form appeared. It was rushing toward me. Behind it, on the other side of the fence, the horses screamed once more. My breath caught, my heart stopped, my mind flashed to Bob, sleeping snugly in the house. Why did I let him sleep? He should be out here. Doing this. Being brave. Like me. Standing my ground. Not screaming. I tried to run. I tried to say something. Mouth. Feet. Nothing would cooperate.

The apparition bumped me. It whinnied pitifully. One of the colts. Outside the fence. Terrified. Separated from its mother. I recognized Chancy's call from beyond the gate. Her baby.

"Well, Mac," I said, when I was finally able to speak, "so it's you causing all this commotion. Your namesake would be ashamed of you. He'd never get into a situation like this."

Micah's hero, TV's McGyver. Micah's horse, Mac.

Now everything exploded into action. Here was help. Here was comfort. Here was an excuse to act ridiculous. The horses inside the fence began screaming again, running in circles. Mac leaped away from me, ran into the woods, ran back, ran into the fence, ran around me. Obediah decided to get into the act. He started barking and running around. Everybody was excited. Crash into me. Nudge my hand. Hurry, hurry.

I was not happy. One shoe had come off. The other was buried past the top in mud. Or something. I tried not to think about it.

At last, the horses were all reunited and I was in the moonlight again, heading toward the house. Bob was coming out the door. He realized that I wasn't with him. Had missed me. I felt somewhat mollified.

"Any trouble?" he asked.

"Not much."

I cleaned up, crawled back into bed, closed my eyes.

No! The fire department was being called. I leaped, almost, out of bed. Ran down the stairs, started getting my gear on before I realized it was an EMS call. Not for me. I'm just a fireman. Not medical. Wearily, I dragged back up the stairs, crawled back into bed, closed my eyes.

Outside a cat screamed, then another. Obediah thundered down the stairs. He hit the ground outside barking, challenging.

"It's so easy to get a good night's deep sleep out here in the country," our guests rhapsodized the next morning. "It's so peaceful and quiet and restful. No wonder you are all so healthy."

"We love it," I yawned, while trying to smooth the bags out from under my eyes. "The peacefulness, I mean."

Conquering the Hills of Duluth

The world just dropped out of sight. All I could see was the blue sky and little white clouds below me. I slammed on the brakes.

"What's wrong?" Sharon gasped.

"Where'd everything go?" I demanded in a panic. "How did we get up so high?"

"Up high? Oh!" Sharon laughed. "That's not the sky. That's Lake Superior waving at you. Just follow the highway down around that curve."

"Mrs. Hodge," the little Girl Scouts began squealing, "people are sure giving you dirty looks."

I glanced at the cars whipping around us, the drivers were indeed looking disagreeable. I eased off the clutch and slowly inched the car along the steep curve.

Sharon and I were taking our Girl Scout troop to the Duluth Zoo. It had seemed like a good idea a few weeks before; but it had been a long, long time since I had driven in big city traffic. I had never driven in a city with vertical streets. We finally reached the bottom of the curve, and then I almost fainted. Instead of finding a proper city with proper city streets, we were staring straight down, what seemed, an even steeper street. I was surprised that the car was not flipping end over end.

"Don't panic girls!" I cried out to the back of the car, "but we are all going to die."

Giggles and shouts of appreciation at this unplanned excitement greeted this statement. I shrugged and allowed the car to roll on to the bottom of the abyss. We finally landed on a level street. That's when Sharon pointed out that we were too far north. That was fine with me, because south was still on level ground. We enjoyed the zoo and later explored the edges of Lake Superior. I dawdled as much as I could, postponing as long as possible, the return trip. I knew, beyond doubt, that I would never get up those hills alive.

"Well, girls," I said, as I turned the key, that started the engine, that turned the wheels, that would soon attack the hills. "We are going to have to be very, very quiet".

Everyone got very, very quiet.

"When we start up those mountainous steeps," I said, "Everyone must lean forward."

"Why?" somebody wanted to know.

"It's a lesson in physics," I explained, carefully. "It's called gravity. See, we will soon be defying the laws of gravity, and if we lean back on the seats, the G-forces will displace the air in the cushions and, 'Eureka,' we'll all have to run down the street naked, and then we'll be arrested for breaking the law," I finished.

"What law?"

"The law of gravity, of course" Sharon quipped.

The girls sat in stunned silence, leaning forward. They knew we weren't serious, but they were't taking any chances.

I began cruising the streets, looking for one that seemed reasonable. I couldn't find one that seemed reasonable.

"Okay girls, hang on!" I shouted as I turned the car to face upward. "Here we go!"

I floored the accelerator and we began to climb.

"Lean forward more," Sharon cried out. "We are going to make it."

We all began to chant "We're going to make it, we're going to make it, we're going to make it, we're going to…aaaggghhh!" I cried. "A stop sign. Someone put a stop sign on top of this mountain pass."

I jammed both feet on the clutch and brake so hard; I nearly slid forward off the seat. Now we were all hanging upside down at the top of a hill in a strange city where no one knew us. What would they do with our remains? Would they leave us in the lake?

"I can't do it, Sharon," I said through clenched teeth. "If I once let off this clutch, we're done for. This little car can't get going fast enough."

"You can do it," Sharon encouraged. "Come on. I've got confidence in you, kid."

I was breathing pretty fast. Any minute now, I would hyperventilate and pass out.

"Mrs. Hodge, look, a policeman!"

Sharon and I both jumped. My feet slipped off both pedals and we started rolling backward.

Shrieks and screams filled the air and just as suddenly stopped. The car rocked, as I slammed it to a teeth rattling halt. I looked in the rear-view mirror. The driver of the car behind us was a woman. The woman was smiling.

"Smile, lady," I thought. "Little do you know," and then an evil thought flittered through my mind. "If her car is directly behind us, then I can roll backward only that far. I won't fall off the edge of Duluth."

Confident now, I quickly let off the brake, crushed down on the gas pedal and released the clutch. A roar and a surge and we were up and over and across and, oh no! I had taken the wrong lane and we were heading down hill again.

The second time at the stop sign, I had lost most of my terror. "I beat you before," I said grimly, "and I'll beat you again."

"How come that policeman is still there?" One of the girls asked, just as I was executing my foolproof, topping the mountain, routine. This time, though, I stayed left and we were heading for home.

"The reason the policeman was still there," I expounded to the girls as we traveled along, "was for our protection. As a servant of the taxpayer, he was waiting to make certain that we would be all right."

"The reason that the policeman was still there," Sharon corrected, "Was because he was in no condition to drive."

"Huh?"

"He was laughing so hard at our antics, he couldn't see."

Snake! Snake!

"Surely, you don't intend to bring that gun with you?" I asked Bob.

"Yes, I certainly do intend to carry, 'that gun,'" he answered emphatically. "How do you expect me to get any target practice if I leave it in the truck?"

"Well, can't you disguise it or something? It's embarrassing. What if someone comes driving by, and here you are walking along like 'The Rifleman', or something? Can't you at least hide it with a towel?"

"Look, Dear," Bob said patiently, "at this time in history, in the state of Texas, it is against the law to carry a concealed weapon. Do you want me to go to jail?"

"No."

"Well then."

"Well, I'll still be embarrassed if you carry it out in the open. Why don't you wait and come out here with your brothers, and practice some other day? When I'm not around."

Bob is usually pretty easy going, so he left the gun in the truck, locked both doors, and we walked off along the road, looking at bluebonnets and enjoying the quiet Texas countryside. There wasn't a house for miles.

We passed a particularly gnarled mesquite tree and Bob, absolutely, had to wade through waist deep weeds to get a better look at its twisted branches. I stayed on the road.

Now, copperhead snakes are not vicious. They would rather run than fight, if they can get away. When Bob, unknowingly, stepped down on the peacefully sleeping copperhead, it just shot right out from under his boot as far as it could. Unfortunately, when it got to the end of its tail, it couldn't go any farther. Bob was standing on it, his boot heel pinning it to the ground.

He felt the commotion under his foot and looked down just in time to see the snake coming back to retrieve its tail. That's when Bob let out a war whoop, and jumped straight up, clearing at least three and a half feet. He looked like he was flying.

"Snake!" he yelled.

"Sssssnake! I'll get the gun." I dashed up the hill to the truck and grabbed the door handle. It was locked. Bob had the key. What to do, what to do. Frantically, I looked in the back of the truck and, what joy! A hoe. I grabbed it and dashed back down to my poor, defenseless husband, who was thrashing down the weeds with a stick, watching for the snake.

"I couldn't get the gun, but here's a hoe," I cried out, breathlessly.

"Good," he shouted, "quick, bring it here."

Full stop!

Take it there? In those weeds? With a known snake in there?

"Look here, Mr. Hodge, Sir! If you want this here now hoe. You are going to have to come and get it yourself." Absolute rebellion.

Much later, when we had determined that the snake had safely escaped to the next county, and we were driving back home, we talked about the adventure.

"Weren't you proud of me, Dear? I mean, no one had to tell me to get the gun. I just ran after it all on my own."

"Um hmm," Bob said.

"And then, when I couldn't get into the truck, I had the presence of mind to get the hoe. That was really thinking, wasn't it?"

"Yeah, you were really thinking."

I could see that he wasn't pleased about my not taking him the hoe.

"Well," I said, "what if the situation were reversed, and I was the one being attacked by a snake? What would you do then?"

"If a snake ever tried to bite you, Dear, you can be assured, that I would do everything in my power to help you."

That sounded good. Naturally, when the situation did come up, Bob was away at work.

Someone to Watch Over Me

"Don't be afraid," the star of the show said, "no one here is going to bite you, but him, and him, and her, and me."

Laughter.

I nervously crushed my fingers together.

"What key do you sing in?" the director/ pianist asked.

"Key?" I said.

"All right," he said soberly. "You just start singing away, and I'll pick up with you. Okay?"

I began to really get nervous. Though I had dreamed of this audition for weeks, I had not been prepared with a song. Somewhere, in the back of, what I laughingly refer to as, my mind, I had just assumed that they would say, "Great. You're in!" or some such, and I would be in the big show. This, of course, would happen without so much as a minute of preparation on my part. I was fifteen.

"What should I sing?"

I could see that the members of the cast were getting just a little put out at me. I got even more nervous.

It was all my mother's fault. She should have made me practice a song. The fact that we didn't have a piano didn't help. The fact that I couldn't read music didn't help much either. Mom should have been more prepared. After all, she was the one who had heard about the audition. I had to do the hard part.

"Do you know…" his fingers began running over the piano keys, making beautiful sounds… "This?"

"No," I shook my head sadly.

"How about…," he began another song.

"Yes!" I almost shouted. "I've heard it somewhere."

The star sang it through for me a few times and I was on my own. It was a perfect choice. After all, I was already half of thirty, and not married. My parents, of course, labored under the delusion of college and career for me, but I already knew what I wanted.

"…someone to watch over me," I sang with all my heart.

I passed the audition. I was in the show. Now, at home, I changed from being an unbearable teenager, to being an obnoxious, insufferable, unbearable teenager.

During rehearsals, away from family, I was too sweet for words. Also, a little too dumb for words. Since I was the youngest of the cast, I got preferential treatment. I also got left out of most of the conversations. That didn't stop me. No sir. When everyone else laughed, I laughed. If someone looked angry, I, also, was riled. I was an adult now. I had conquered the highest of heights.

I looked down on my classmates at school. Poor common kids. And my parents, poor things, just didn't realize that I was so much more in touch with the world than they. Oh, it was a lonely life.

The director put me in a few spots and gave me a solo. Naively, I felt that the backup singers and musicians were being favored to perform with me. It was many years before I discovered just how important backup is to a singer.

The song was a happy, catchy tune; lively, and calculated to make people snap their fingers, or clap their hands, or, at least, tap their feet. My mom and dad listened to me morning and night. For weeks. Their nerves must have very nearly snapped. Their hands were constantly clapped over their ears. Their feet stopped tapping and started running to another room whenever I entered, singing.

At last, the big night!

There we were. Getting ready for the show. The glamorous backstage. We were in the dressing room. Ho, ho, I was wearing heavy make-up. Lots and lots of really, dark, heavy make-up!

Someone came to the door. Knock. Knock. We all turned. It was a Very Important Man. He had flowers for the star. She thanked him sweetly. Make a note, I thought. For when it's my turn. Nobody brought me flowers. That was okay. After all, no one had heard me sing. Yet. Next time.

My parents had said, "no next time," but they would change their minds. When they realized how mature I had become, due solely to this opportunity, they would surely change their minds.

The show started. We all danced out for the big intro. We performed our various acts and skits. The dancers danced. The emcee told jokes. The pianist played. All went very well. At last, my big solo. I did it. No mistakes. With the applause still resounding, I reeled back to the dressing room, barely able to function, as I fumblingly changed into my next costume. I had made it! Fame! Fortune! Let no one refer to me as a child. I was going to be a star. Show biz and me!

There was a big cast party afterward. I got to eat all the hamburgers and fries that I wanted. Umm! I got to drink my first sip of champagne. "Delightful," I lied. I couldn't think why anyone would want to drink vinegar, but I was mature. I said it tasted wonderful. They wouldn't let me have more. I pretended to be upset.

It was one o'clock in the morning. I was at a party. The youngest there. If only my parents didn't ruin it by insisting that I leave before everyone else. Maybe I should quit school. Maybe I should move out on my own. Certainly, I had proved that I was quite capable of taking care of myself.

There was someone beside my chair. I glanced up. One of the band members stood there. He asked me to dance. My heart nearly stopped. He reminded me of the gorgeous, the sophisticated, Peter Lawford. He walked, I glided, out to the dance floor.

The music was soft now. We began to dance. Me! Dancing with a mature man. A man that looked like a handsome movie star. If only the kids at school could see me now. I leaned my head against his chest. I closed my eyes. I fell asleep.

On the Block

"Twenty-five. Twenty-five."

"Twenty-five?" My lips moved silently, in disbelief, my eyes were glued to the television set. "Twenty-five thousand dollars?"

I was watching a live telecast of a cattle auction. It was hard to convince myself that the people that I was watching were actually real. I knew there were lots of people out there with more money than they needed; this, this, was ludicrous.

"Bob, you should have seen them. I mean, they were just dripping with diamonds and gold and silks and satins," I paused to let that sink into his mind's-eye, "and you should have seen the women. They were really dressed up, too."

He smiled indulgently. Bob had seen auctions like this before. He had been to them, watching people bid for animals for several hundred thousand dollars each. It was staggering.

"Do you know how they bid?" I whispered.

He nodded his head. He knew. That didn't stop me. I told him anyway.

"They didn't say a word. They just sat there and when they wanted to bid another ten grand or so, they would just sit there. And, Honey, they didn't even raise their hand or any such like that. They barely, almost imperceptibly, tilted their head. And that was a bid. Poof! Ten thousand dollars."

"Yes, Dear," Bob soothed, "That's the way the other side does it.

"What would happen," I asked darkly, "if they didn't have the money? Or changed their minds? Or if they were only looking down at their hands or at the floor or something? Huh? What would happen then?"

Bob looked very, very serious. "That is something not spoken of in their circles. The penalty would be unbearable. No one," he intoned, "goes to that type of auction without realizing the ultimate price that they would have to pay for reneging on a bid."

"You mean they die?" I breathed, horrified.

Bob didn't answer, he just smiled mysteriously and went off to work on the car.

Not too many weeks after that, he asked me if I wanted to go to an auction. I told him sure. It wasn't for rich people, he said, just for the commoners.

"Like us?" I asked.

"Well, not quite that common," he replied.

Unlike the televised auction, this one just had a few flashes of gold and diamonds, mostly on the women. The men wore tailored western cut suits and five hundred dollar boots. I felt just a little out of place.

"Now don't move your arm or hand or anything," Bob warned.

Apparently these people were on the lower strata of the elite. They actually made slight motions with their hands to make a bid. The bids were peanuts, really. Nothing more than five thousand dollars at a time.

I didn't blink an eye. I didn't move a muscle. I didn't even breathe. All other clichés are pertinent here. I was scared to death.

We didn't bid on anything and we got out of there alive and well, with our integrity, and our checkbook intact.

"I don't like auctions," I told Bob. "I can't stand the strain."

He just laughed.

Several years later, our youth organization was having a bake sale and auction. I bought goodies right off the table, spent all my money, and sat back, pleased with myself for doing my part and yet not getting caught up in the part that I didn't like.

"Mrs. Hodge," a child from our group said, sliding up to my side. "If you see my mother, will you tell her that I went downstairs to change clothes?"

"Sure," I said, "Where is she?"

"Over there somewhere," she said, and ran off toward the stairs.

"What was that all about?" a friend, sitting next to me, wanted to know.

I explained.

"I don't see her though," I said, standing up and scanning the other side of the auditorium. "Oh, there she is. I see her."

I waved my arm frantically, to catch her attention. Too late, I realized where I was.

“Eleven dollars,” the young auctioneer shouted gleefully as he pointed to me. “I’ve got eleven dollars.”

“Gasp! No!” I shouted back for all the world to see and hear. I whipped my arm down to my side, then raised both arms and whisked them back and forth in front of my scarlet colored face to signal a negated bid. I didn’t have a penny in my purse.

“That’s only the rich guys that have to pay the ‘ultimate’ price for reneging on a bid. Right, Bob?” I asked when I got home. I explained the situation to him.

He assured me that all would be well.

I believe him, too. I mean, what’s eleven dollars? It was just an honest mistake, after all. There’s no need to keep glancing over my shoulder. What’s to worry?

Haw! Gee! and Mush!

Socrates, apparently, had mixed emotions about our dog sled. When I took the blue harness off the peg, his whole, eighty-five plus pounds of, mostly St. Bernard body would quiver with anticipation. Outside, he would race madly around the sled, keeping just out of reach. He would bounce in front of me, his forepaws flat on the ground, his tail wigwaging a special "ah, come on. Let's just go for a walk. We don't need that old sled," message.

After much ado, I would harness him to the sled, set four-year-old Rebekah to be the passenger, and take my place behind.

"Let's go, Socrates! On, you great husky." I said this even though he wasn't a Husky. I also said things like, "Gee!" and, "Haw!" and, I'd even yell the unauthentic, "Mush!" just to feel important, in an obscure, *Call of the Wild,* sort of way.

Some thought that all of this would confuse poor Socrates. They needn't have worried. He had his own pattern for pulling a sled, or rather, abstaining from pulling a sled. Halfway up the driveway, he would collapse. His legs would splay out in four different directions, then, when I dragged him back together again, he'd roll onto his back, loll his tongue out one side of his mouth, and pant loudly.

"Socrates," I would yell, "You are useless. You are lazy. You are, undoubtedly, the most despicably worthless animal in the whole world."

Socrates had a, "sticks and stones," philosophy, apparently. He would just lay there, upside down, grinning at me.

I would drag him to his feet and hurry to my place behind the sled. Then, by pushing and bumping him, I could get him to swing into the spirit of it all, and between the two of us we would get the sled to the top of the driveway and turn to face down the road to the bridge. Then Socrates would put on a burst of speed and we would rocket down the road. I would jump on the runners and he would turn, leap high into the air, and jump on the sled, very nearly on Rebekah's lap. Then, amidst shrieks and laughs and barks, we would sail past our mailbox. He and Rebekah were oblivious to the fact that two humans and a dog, all riding on a runaway sled, might seem a bit unusual.

There was only one time that Socrates willingly pulled the sled, using his own energy. We were trying to get back from the bridge, and had managed to make it to our mailbox. I saw Sharon standing beside her snowmobile at the bottom of our driveway. She had come for a surprise visit. I waved to her and urged the reluctant Socrates onward. He was upset because we had already established that I would not push the sled up the hill, while he rode on the front like some great potentate leading his minions. Sharon sized up the situation pretty accurately, and called out to him.

Perhaps he was showing off, perhaps he recognized her as the gal who brought homemade cookies. Whatever the reason, Socrates suddenly tore into action. He raced up the hill toward our driveway so fast, I could barely hold onto the sled. Turning down our driveway, he doubled his speed. All I could do was hang on, to keep the sled from tipping and spilling Rebekah onto the packed, hard driveway. I couldn't make my feet go fast enough. They were touching the ground about every six yards, and that was only after the rest of me had already gone by.

Just as we got to the halfway point, Socrates whirled, made a spectacular leap into the air and landed gracefully onto the sled and Rebekah. We swooped past Sharon, my feet at last on the runners. Socrates barked, Rebekah shouted, and I jauntily waved my hat. We slowed to a stop just past the hitching rail.

"What was that all about?" Sharon asked in awe.

"Team work," I told her.

Pie Aren't Squared

The only worthwhile interest of first grade, as far as I could see, was learning to read. All else left me totally in a fog. I was amazed that other children understood what was going on. I was more amazed that my parents, who claimed to love me, sent me off each day to be fussed at by some strange woman, for not paying attention. After awhile, I caught onto the lesson of cause and effect. I decided to pay attention. I even tried to take part.

My first sharing time was a real flop. Everyone was interested when I told the class about running into the nearest establishment for shelter when a man tried to entice me into his car. When I confided to one and all that the establishment was a bar, the teacher expressed firm disapproval. When I tried to justify my fear of the man by mentioning the gun he was hiding "Under his arm," (my best ability to describe my first encounter with a shoulder holster), I was banished back to my desk in shame.

Over the ensuing years, I really did try to pay attention. It was hard. Mostly I wandered around various subjects in a daze, wondering what was wrong with me. I was miserable and barely managed to pass from one grade to the next.

To me the most important things in life were reading, riding, (bike), and playing Cowboys and Indians. Dolls were okay, but that was awfully tame. School was prison.

Once, when a sailor came to our school, I was intrigued by the statement, that they must wear rubber-soled shoes so that they would not slip overboard and drown. Enthusiastically, I raised my hand and asked if they would float for a long time, because they were wearing rubber-soled shoes. Goofed again. I really was trying. My teachers seemed to feel that way about me, too.

I became a survivalist. If you don't raise your hand, and you don't fail the tests, the teachers, mostly, forget that you are there and you are free to spend your valuable time daydreaming about more important matters. I rarely raised my hand. I rarely failed a test. It worked very well.

Then came the end of a beautiful system. In junior-high, they gave us all a special test. The test wasn't so hard. The aftereffects were disastrous. My parents were called to the school. A major powwow was called consisting of teachers, principal, guidance counselor and me. It was terrible.

Words and numbers were bandied about. The words, "Bored," and "Challenging," were flung back and forth from teacher to teacher. They were planning my life. They were going to make me use my brain. They were going to make me work.

"The test wasn't hard," I told them, desperately. "It was just stuff I already knew."

They looked at one another and smiled knowingly.

"I read it in books. It's just that I read a lot. I read anything, encyclopedias and ketchup bottles and comic books and, and, just stuff." I felt like falling on my knees. Please don't label me. I didn't want to be challenged in school. I didn't want to look like Albert Einstein with flyaway white hair. I didn't want to have to think. To reason. Help!

There was no help. They all decided that I had to be challenged. Algebra I, was part of the answer. I toyed very seriously with the idea of running away. Reluctantly, I entered the world of Algebra I.

I hated it. "A," was a letter. "Two, was a number." Why confuse the issue? I grew sullen and refused to pay attention. The teacher pleaded, cajoled, threatened, to no avail. My rebellion was complete; until one day, when she said something really interesting.

I had been sitting at the desk, gazing off into space, when I was suddenly jolted back to earth by her statement.

"Pie are squared."

"Really? How can that be?" I wondered. I pulled my pencil and paper together and drew a pie. It was definitely round. Usually it was cut into wedges. Maybe she meant two pies. No, she had definitely said, "Pie," singular. The trick here was to discover why a person would say, "Pie are squared."

I began to draw. Suddenly, I understood. Algebra was fascinating after all. I dragged out protractor and compass. I had it! I looked up proudly into the eyes of the instructor.

"Do you have it?" she asked.

I nodded, beaming.

"Why don't you share it on the board?" She was excited.

I swaggered to the front of the class, picked up the chalk and began to draw.

"The catch to the whole thing," I explained, "is the knowledge of proper English."

I began to grid off my pie. "If we say, 'pie IS squared,' we would have to somehow; make this pie into a square. It can't be done. But, pie ARE squared, simply means that we cut this pie into many, tiny, even, square pieces, giving us the plural, 'are'. We could expand it into the more difficult, 'pie are cubed,' but that would entail discovering just how deep the pie are."

I glanced at the teacher. She didn't seem too happy.

I flunked Algebra I.

The educators of that school must have lost faith in the testing and evaluating system of our society.

I have long since learned that flyaway white hair does not a genius make. Mostly, though, I have learned that life goes on, and the less you know, the better off you be.

Lifeguard Training

"If we are going to be spending a lot of time at the lake this summer," I told Bob, "One of us needs to take lifeguard training."

Bob agreed. Since it's pretty common knowledge that a mommy with four children has more spare time than a daddy with a full time job, it was decided that I would be the one to achieve the honors.

The following Tuesday night I was standing beside an enormous indoor swimming pool with more than a dozen nineteen to twenty-four year old men. The only other woman in sight was our instructor; an extremely large woman, with an authoritative voice and an Army sergeant's bearing. I was awed. So was everyone else in the class.

She handed out books for us to read and lectured us on how important we were going to be to our community, our families and to ourselves. It was very inspiring.

"This is going to be so easy," I told Bob later. "We just have to swim around the pool for awhile, using varying strokes. It'll be a breeze."

The next Tuesday we got into more details. We learned about Struggling and Overcoming Struggling. We learned that, contrary to popular opinion, the Red Cross does not advocate socking your victim in the face for his own good. As the weeks went on we all became very adept at lifesaving.

One night the instructor came in with an armload of bricks.

"Tonight," she proclaimed, "you will save these bricks from downing."

"Do we give them mouth-to-mouth resuscitation?" One of the bolder boys wanted to know.

"Do you want I should give you brick-to-mouth?" She shot back.

He just smiled, weakly.

All around me, slim, lean, young men swam out to the deepest part of the pool, surface-dived to the bottom, and proceeded to rescue their respective brick victims.

I swam out to the deepest part of the pool, surface-dived to about four feet and popped back up to the top.

"I can't seem to get down to the bottom of the pool," I complained.

"Yeah," our instructor agreed, "You've got the same problem I have. B.B:"

"B.B?"

"Buoyant Bottom," she laughed.

That did it! I swam back out, jack-knifed under and somehow managed to get hold of that poor, half-drowned brick. I deposited it perilously close to the instructor's bare toes.

"Very good," she laughed. "See what you can do when you really want to," she laughed again, "You do what you have to do."

Testing was soon upon us and things seemed to be going very well. The written test was really too easy. Then we had to demonstrate various life-saving methods. Throwing buoys and ropes, reaching out to the victims with sticks or towels; doing anything but coming into actual, physical contact with the drowning victim.

Struggling and Overcoming Struggling was the last test.

Two victims, a burly Marine sergeant and a fifty-four year-old-lady swimming instructor, were sent to the deep end of the pool, and told to drown.

Four students were lined up to rescue the Marine. The rest lined up for their turn to rescue the L.O.L.

"Go!" Our instructor yelled, and two students jumped into the pool. With clean, quick strokes, they approached the two victims, who were floundering and thrashing about in the water, screaming to be saved.

Both students jack-knifed underwater. We saw the marine spin around and disappear underneath the surface for a split second as the student's right arm snaked across his chest. Placidly, he allowed himself to be towed to the edge of the pool.

The other student was having a problem. When he dived under to grab his victim's legs, and turn her around, she kicked him in the chest. Then she reached down, grabbed his hair, and jerked him out of the water. She screamed frantically into his face, then, before he could get over the shock of all this, plunged him back underwater and proceeded to stand on his head.

Everyone melted into the line to go save the marine.

"Get back into two lines, you cowards," shouted our instructor.

Soon it was my turn.

"Put a little excitement into it," the instructor ordered my victim.

He did. Before I got near enough to him to dive under the water, he lunged forward and grabbed me around the neck. We sank straight down. I kicked and tried to pry his hands free. All that accomplished was a stronger, tighter hold. We were swirling underwater now and he was slowly squeezing, what little breath I had…out. I was going to drown. During a test. Right under the noses of all these lifeguards. I was going to drown.

There was one last resort. I took it. I opened my mouth and sank my teeth into the soft part of his shoulder.

"Yagghhh!" he screamed, as he threw his arms upward and lifted out of the water. "She bit me!"

There, sure enough, were two half-circles of near blood. I hadn't meant to bite that hard.

"Darlene," our instructor scowled, "the Red Cross frowns on their lifeguards maiming their victims."

"I only did what I had to do," I told her innocently.

She laughed. "Go try again," she told us.

He swam away from me and half-heartedly cried out for help.

Warily, I swam toward him. There was little need for caution, though. Before I got to within five feet of him, he flipped over and floated on his back. "Help," he said softly. "Help, help."

As I had told Bob in the beginning, the class was a breeze.

Reluctant Decoy

Prowler problems were plaguing our neighborhood. The authorities in the city where we lived were unable to correct the problem, and the only solution seemed to be a vigilante committee.

"We've decided, Darlene," they informed me, "that you'll be a decoy."

"Who? Me?"

They had it all planned. I would stay overnight at a neighbor's house, dress in the husband's work clothes, and drive off in his car, just as he did every morning at four-thirty. The prowler would, no doubt, be fooled, try to break in and the neighbor man would be there to catch him. Then all the other men in the neighborhood would dash over and help hold him for the police. A great plan.

"Why me?" I wanted to know.

"Because you're closest to his size."

I glanced at him. He was very short. Tall, thin Bob couldn't do it, and neither could the other men in the neighborhood. I sighed.

"Okay," I said.

The evening of the Great Plan arrived. I kissed my loved ones good-bye and left the house.

"Be careful," they said, "don't take any chances."

Take chances? Hah! Not me!

I didn't get a great deal of sleep that short night; and I didn't realize just how very dark it can be at four-thirty in the morning. Five minutes before departure found the three of us sitting around the kitchen table, whispering, nibbling on dry toast, and drinking strong, black coffee.

I had prayed for a slight earthquake or even a little tornado. Not enough to hurt anyone, just enough to give me an excuse to go home.

At first, I thought that the coffee sloshing out of my cup was the beginning of the answer to my prayers. Funny, I thought, it's just the coffee in my cup that's spilling…and my hands that are shaking…and my heart that's thumping so loud…

"There's nothing to worry about," the neighbor lady assured me.

"That's right," her husband agreed. "It's all under control."

"Well, if it's all under control," I said, reasonably, "why are we all talking in whispers?"

They just smiled.

"Look," the husband said, "Bob's watching from your house across the street, and there are two other men watching from their homes. Nothing's going to happen, except that we are going to catch this character and turn him over to the police. Simple."

Sure, I thought. Simple.

I began gathering my props. I put on the man's jacket and hat, picked up his lunch pail, and went to the door.

"Remember to quick check the car, to make sure that he's not in there," they warned.

I wouldn't forget. If he was in the car, I was to drive out of the garage slowly, and Bob and the others would rush the car and save me. If the car happened to be empty of evil doers, I was to zoom out the driveway in the husband's usual manner. I was to head straight for Bob's sister's house.

"This job is full of holes," I whined.

"Piece of cake," they said in unison.

"Here's your cigarette," the man of the house said.

"What's that for?" I gasped.

"I always walk out with a cigarette in my hand. If you don't carry one, he might get suspicious."

"Oh," I took the cigarette. He moved back behind the door. I stepped out. Alone. Into the night.

I knew I was in trouble as soon as I opened the car door. They had fixed the interior light so the guy couldn't see me when I got into the car. It was a great idea, except for a slight problem for me. If he was in there, I couldn't see him either.

I also couldn't see the ignition switch. I scraped the key along the steering column, and then along the dashboard. In desperation, I put the smoldering cigarette between my teeth and clamped down, hard. I kept glancing toward the rearview mirror, hoping that I wouldn't see anything.

My heart began banging around so hard, if there had been someone in the back seat, I wouldn't have been able to hear him, even if he had shouted in my ear.

The tip of the cigarette began to glow brighter. That surprised me. It was bobbing up and down so fast, I couldn't understand why it hadn't gone out. Ashes began to flutter off into space and I worried about setting the car afire. I suppressed a cough and wiped the smoke induced tears from my eyes.

I found the switch! I turned the key and the car roared to life, the sound reverberated throughout the garage. Carefully now, I eased the gearshift into drive and the car slowly rolled forward.

The smoke seemed to be curling out of my ears by this time, and I was feeling dizzy, and queasy, and ready to expire. I tried to cough gently. A great gasp of a cough exerted itself, and the cigarette flew toward the windshield. I slapped it back and yelped in surprise and pain as the glowing tip burned my hand and lips. Startled, I let my foot slip and slammed down on the accelerator. The car rocketed down the driveway, while I coughed and choked and tried to wipe my eyes. I swerved sharply to keep from running into my house, across the way, and careened down the street, wondering if the bad guy was in the car with me, or if he had walked into our trap.

My sister-in-law sat quietly, watching as I peeled the crushed cigarette off my face and teeth. She gave me a cup of coffee and repeated the gist of the phone call from Bob. The plan had worked.

"That was pretty brave," she said, "being a decoy like that."

"Nothing to it," I told her, pretending to dismiss the praise, "all I did was drive a car over here. It was nothing."

She was impressed.

S'nicker

Minny Soda, our beautiful coal-black horse, was doing her best to play a trick on one of her barnyard neighbors.

We were standing, Bob and I, with our arms folded across the top of the gate next to the barn. The farm menagerie that we had acquired over the years often entertained us. We enjoyed watching their antics. We had, long ago, decided that those who claim animals don't think or that they have no personalities, must have not OBSERVED animals, at least, not ours.

Clearly, Minny had something in mind. She, apparently, was on a mission.

The goats were intent on exploring the fence line, looking for a means of escape. The chickens were scattered about scratching up tasty morsels for themselves. The cows, and Minny's mother, Second Chance, were warily watching the rakish young equine.

Several chickens had found a promising area to their interest. They were very busy, heads bobbing up and down, their tails up, and feathers spread to keep an even balance.

Minny Soda had picked her victim, a big, plump hen, totally engrossed in minding her own business. She, too, had her tail feathers fanned out, and had turned her south end, going north, to the barn door.

Slowly, softly, carefully, Minny eased herself forward from the barn, her broad, black nose nearly bumping the ground. Her ears were pointed toward the hen. She really did look as though she was doing her best to tiptoe.

We watched, enchanted, as she moved closer and closer. Then she was directly behind her target, and slowly, deliberately, she raised her nose, just slightly.

"Awk! Squawk!" The hen, wings flapping, beak agape, dignity destroyed, rose straight to the roof of the goat shed. There, accompanied by her peers, she, and they, continued the harangue as Minny jumped, whirled on her hind legs, whinnied loudly and galloped off, her long, black mane and tail flying.

Chancy, taking her cue from all the excitement, reared, nickered several times, then raced after her daughter through the field and into the woods. She, in turn, was followed by the goats, who thundered after them in wild ecstasy at this new form of entertainment.

The horses, goats, dogs, and even the milk cows raced, and called in their respective manner, all over the south field, obviously enjoying the excuse to act unmitigatedly silly.

Later, Minny Soda came trotting back to the barn. She nuzzled Bob's cupped hand.

"Hhhhrrrrrrhhhhhh," she murmured and nodded her head against his chest.

"You're something else, Minny," he laughed.
Minny snickered. Obviously, she agreed.

I Helped

"She come here from Russia, young girl, alone. Long time ago," the priest told the assemblage of mourners, in his charming Serbian accent. "She has nice family. She has good life." He continued on, a wonderful eulogy of my grandmother and her life in America.

One good/bad process about living in a small, transplanted, European community, is that everyone knows everyone, if not by sight, then by their life happenings.

My mother married outside the community, and we lived in a different part of the country. My dad was in the Air Force so, actually, we lived in many different parts of the country. However, when we go back for a visit, I am still, simply, Sophie's daughter.

This accepted method of identification actually does save a great deal of trouble and long introductions during weddings, funerals and parades.

Uncles and aunts and cousins, the whole ménage was there at the funeral, except for one of my cousins.

The eldest grandson. He and his family had gone travel camping in the Dakotas, and no one knew exactly where they were. The highway patrol had been contacted to get a message to them, but to no avail. We knew that they would be broken hearted, but there was nothing that could be done.

After the funeral, friends and family had all gathered in the basement of the church. I was trying to be on my very best behavior.

"Remember," I had told the children, "a good name is important and we don't want to do or say anything that would sully your great-grandmother's memory. Stand tall. Be polite. Act like little ladies and gentlemen."

We were all doing exceptionally well. I impressed quite a few people with little one-liners in Serbian, and Bob was doing very well, too. It hadn't taken him long to learn to introduce himself as "Sophie's son-in-law."

"Where are the other grandchildren?" one of my grandmother's contemporaries inquired softly.

Carefully, I pointed out various cousins as we surveyed the room.

"That tall man there, is the oldest boy's second son," I said, "and there is his wife and, oh, two of their children." I faithfully gave information that would make my grandmother proud of all her family. No black sheep. No siree!

"Isn't there someone missing?" the lady asked.

"Oh, yes. The oldest grandchild. Well, he's not here. You see, he's out in a boat, in Dakota." I struggled not to get too involved in an explanation. My Serbian and her English were really not up to involved explanations. "He's camping out," I explained. "On vacation."

"During his grandmother's funeral, he's on vacation?"

"Well, he doesn't know, you see."

"Nobody called him?"

"No, he's out in the wilderness somewhere."

Just then another lady joined us.

"The oldest grandson is not here," lady number one told her.

"Oh?"

"He's gone to Dakota," I explained, lamely.

"Why?"

How to explain, without making my cousin appear uncaring about his own grandmother? The ladies were both eyeing me suspiciously. I just had to protect my grandmother's good name. This was serious business.

"Well," I said gravely, trying to think on my feet. "They'll find him soon. You see, the police are looking for him."

How to Milk a Cow

"Let's see, now. Milking stool, milk bucket, cleaning rags, curry comb and brush… and for my hair, a scarf." I gathered the paraphernalia in all of my arms and headed out toward the cow.

"You need all that just to milk a cow?" Bob asked.

"Yep. Oh, thanks for reminding me." I reached out one more arm and grabbed the library book off the table. "This instruction manual."

Bob had commissioned me to seek out and buy a cow. His reasoning: With the size of our family, a cow was a necessity. He didn't have the time, and neither of us had one iota of knowledge concerning dairy cows, ergo: I should do the seeking and purchasing.

Our new cow had arrived. At our little farm. Ready to give us nice, creamy milk for all of our children to drink and grow healthier.

We didn't have a stanchion. Being true blue Americans, we did what our citizenry is noted for: improvisation. We tied her to the back bumper of our truck.

I glanced around at the family, gathered to watch the first execution of the milking of the Hodge Family Milk Cow. Here was a chance to impress everyone with my vast array of newly acquired knowledge and skill. Knowledge from the library book, skill from practicing on a water-filled, rubber glove.

"First one must cover one's head with a scarf or cap or some such," I announced grandly.

I tied the scarf around my head.

"Then one brushes the cow." Gently and carefully, I brushed the cow.

"Now," I looked all around, "the milking."

I sat down on the stool and looked up and up at the cow. My, she was large. Slowly, I began to wring the water from the washing rag and looked at my family. All eyes were following my every move.

"There is one important point that I would like to impress upon you children." I paused to make certain that everyone was paying attention. They were.

"Though we have been visiting many farmers recently, and even though we believe them to be the salt of the earth, so to speak, I want to impress upon you this one truth. We will not avail ourselves of the specific, articulate vernacular that they ascribe to, when discussing various animal anatomy or by-products."

"Huh?" the children said.

"She means don't say the same words that they say," Bob explained.

"Oh," the children grinned.

"Now," I proceeded, "this is the udder. U-d-d-e-r. That's where the milk is. This is the teat. T-e-a-t. That's the faucet that the milk comes out of."

"You ended in a preposition, Mom."

"And spills into the pail," I finished quickly.

"Now." I placed my hands in the proper position. "Watch."

I began the milking process. Nothing happened. I tried again. Still nothing.

"Hee, hee," I said,

I tried again.

Drip. Drip. Two drops of creamy white milk fell into the pail.

I looked up, beaming proudly at my family, who were all beaming proudly back at me. We had entered a new era. We were now real, live farmers. We had milked our first cow.

Some forty-five minutes later, we were all pretty dispirited. Not a quart of milk, and we had all tried hard to milk that cow. We knew that there had to be more milk than that. The book said so.

"Go call Crackers," Bob suggested. "She'll know what to do."

I called the neighbor lady, whom Rebekah had christened, "Crackers."

"Guess what," I told her, "we have a cow."

She's pretty quick-witted and assessed the situation with just those six words. She arrived at our place in less than ten minutes. She finished the milking of our very weary cow in just a few minutes after her arrival.

She gave us some milking lessons and very kindly did not mention "City people."

It didn't take us long to learn about cows. They are gentle. They give lots of milk. They leave a… They give lots of milk. They also slap your face with their tails, but only if their tails are yucky. They give lots of milk. They eat a lot of hay. They give lots of milk. They eat lots of grain. They give lots of milk. Grain costs lots of money. They give lots of milk.

Contrary to popular belief, they do not kick over the milk pail. They wait until the last squirt of milk, and then, very carefully place their entire hind foot into the bucket.

We did not know any of this that first night. We stood looking at our first gallons of milk then. We all dreamed our dreams. It was going to be wonderful. The simple, uncomplicated life was in our grasp.

"Just think, Bob," I whispered, "milking twice a day. All that milk. I can churn butter, and make cheese, and cottage cheese. It will be so peaceful and such fun."

Self Improvement

"Guess what, Honey." I giggled to my husband as I snuggled up beside him on the couch.

"What?"

"You're going to get a brand new wife."

"Why?" he said suspiciously. "I'm content with the one I've got."

"Oh, Silly," I said, delighted with him, "it'll still be me. But, a new me. I'm going to take a charm course and learn to be all beautiful and charming and stuff like that."

Bob just looked at me.

"I'll learn to be graceful, and how to fix my hair, and even the proper clothes to wear."

"The proper clothes?" he said, hopefully. "Really?"

"Yep."

"You mean, no more slouchy blouses and ragged blue jeans?"

"Yep."

"And, no more red shorts with pink and blue tops?"

I looked down at my red shorts and pink and blue oversized blouse. "What's wrong with that? Pink and red are on the same color wheel."

"When do you start this program?" Bob wanted to know.

"Now ladies," our instructor rapped a pencil on the desktop to attract our attention. She seemed very stern.

We all became very, very quiet.

"We are all here for one purpose: because you want to become all that you can. We cannot all be of good breeding. But, it is not necessary for one of lowly birth to advertise the fact.

"Let us not waste time. Though a lady never rushes, she does not waste time. In the next few weeks, I expect to see you accomplishing a great deal, but without any apparent overexertion on your part."

No overexertion? I already had an important ladylike quality, and hadn't even realized it. This was right up my alley. I just knew that I was going to like this course.

The instructor had us all line up, facing her, to accomplish two duties at one time. Introduce ourselves, and practice good posture.

Thus, we would not waste time, do you see.

"Good posture is the hallmark of charm. The absolute essence of beauty," she said, "and the equalizer between women of low and high estate. If there is one fault that makes this instructor positively ill, that one fault is poor posture."

I was impressed. I stood straight and tall. Equal to all and sundry.

She began down the far end of the line and worked her way toward where I stood. Each lady in the class introduced herself as the instructor wrote something in a dainty, little, pink book.

"I'm Darlene Hodge," I told her nervously when it was my turn.

"Hello, Darlene. We're happy to have you in our class. Now let's try standing nice and straight, please," she said primly.

I squared my shoulders to show her that I was already standing nice and straight.

"Oh, my dear," she said, ever so softly, "you must pull your shoulders back. We wouldn't want you to look as though you were carrying a load of coal that you had just picked off the railroad tracks, do we?"

"No," I said hoarsely, as I watched her write something in her dainty, little, pink book.

I wondered if she knew, somehow, that my grandmother had indeed picked coal off the railroad tracks during the Depression. Apparently, my roots were showing. I stood straight and tall. I knew it wouldn't be straight enough or tall enough.

"SOME OF US must practice just an extra bit, with SPECIAL EXERCISES," the instructor said. She turned to the rest of the class.

"Ladies," she told them, "while I'm working with some of the others on, SPECIAL EXERCISES the rest of you practice balancing a book on your head while walking and sitting."

"Now, hmmm, Darlene. Can you do this?"

I watched as she demonstrated the SPECIAL EXERCISES to SOME OF US. Meaning me.

I felt like the middle ring in a circus. It seemed all the other students were more interested in the

SPECIAL EXERCISES portion of the class, than their own assignment.

The instructor kept walking around me, saying, "Hmmm," and "Oh, my," and she kept tsk, tsking. I felt like an elephant in a ballet class. I felt like Quasimodo. I felt like slumping to the floor. I felt like any equalization there might have been for me had dissolved.

I could feel the moisture of that dissolved equalization squeeze out from under my eyelids. I put on my great big, friendliest, toothiest grin.

"Oh, no, no, no," she glanced at her book, "Darlene!"

She turned to the room at large. "Ladies, ladies. Always remember this. A lady never, ever grins. She smiles. A lady's smile does not show teeth. A dog shows teeth. A lady smiles in such a manner that the ends of her lips do not pass the irises of her eyes."

My grin was gone. I bit my lower lip. Instinctively, I knew that a lady's lips never, ever quivered.

"So how was your first day at charm school?" Bob wanted to know that evening.

"Fine."

"Did you hurt your neck, Honey?"

"No, I'm practicing good posture. It's one of our assignments for the week."

"Oh. Are you mad at me?"

"Of course not. Why?"

"Well, you look, er, out of sorts. You don't look too happy."

"Oh, no, that's because you're used to the old me. The lady me is smiling. Like a lady. It's something I learned today."

"So you learned a lot, did you?"

"Oh yes. Lots and lots about myself."

"That's good," Bob patted my head, "I'm glad you had a good time."

I learned something else, too, after I had gotten home. But I didn't tell Bob.

I learned that, if a lady cries while taking a shower, no one will ever know.

Simply Charming

Being ladylike is an acquired ability, I was learning. It seemed to be an awful lot of work. I persevered.

I had decided to improve myself by taking a charm course for women, so that Bob would be proud of me, love me more, and I would become a unique individual, like everyone else.

When we studied the importance of hair styling, I went to beauty shops. They tried all kinds of hairstyles. My instructor was not pleased. I had been going to the wrong places.

I tried patronizing beauty salons, instead. After much consultations, and chopping, and feathering, and piling, my instructor was still not pleased. I persevered.

The rest of the lessons were continually practiced.

I held my head up and my shoulders back. This caused some problems when walking in unfamiliar territory. I stumblingly persevered. Each step was led by my thighs. I no longer stomped around feet foremost, like some common country bumpkin.

I gently reached for, "objects," by leading with the back of my hand. I no longer, "grabbed", for things, I mean "objects."

Meanwhile, my smile was never too wide, nor my lips parted. Laughter was reduced to a ladylike twitter.

When we came to the section about clothes, I thought that the instructor would not make it through, but we both persevered.

"Shakespeare stated that, 'clothes make the man'," she told us, "In this case, I'm sure, he won't mind if we say, 'woman'."

I glanced at a fellow student sitting beside me and smiled. She looked as though she had just swallowed a lemon, so I knew that she was smiling, too.

"A lady always wears hosiery."

Until that time I had ignorantly been wearing nylons. There was so much that I had been doing wrong. Carrying a purse instead of a handbag. Shaking hands with people with a solid, warm grip, instead of just letting my hand be touched. Not smoking.

This last had me mystified. Smoking was ladylike? I needed more information.

"Oh yes," the instructor answered my question. "A cigarette can be used to great advantage. To make one look regal. Sitting with one hand resting beside your knee, a cigarette gently wafting smoke upward between you and the rest of the world, is most elegant. And letting a man light your cigarette for you, while you look up at him through lowered eyelids, is definitely tantalizing."

Tantalizing? Elegant? I frowned.

"But later, how can that be tantalizing or elegant when one is dying from cancer or emphysema?"

"Well, Bob," I said to my husband in a perfectly modulated voice, "today I learned how to insult someone. In a ladylike way, of course."

"Huh?" he said.

"Yes, it's really terrific. What you do, is to look straight at the person, and then, slowly close your eyes as though you are sweeping them away with your eyelashes. Then when you open your eyes, you just look right through the person. As though they weren't there. It's really quite effective." Great drops of liquid welled under my eyelids.

Bob looked at me solemnly.

"Are you enjoying these classes?" he asked.

"Oh sure," I lied, "everyone wants to be a lady."

"Are you absolutely certain that your instructor is one?"

"Of course she is. Well, she says she is. Well, she must be. Don't you think so?"

Bob shook his head. "May I have my old wife back now?" he said quietly.

I sighed and rested my head on his chest.

"Do you mean it's okay with you if I grin, a great big grin, and laugh out loud?"

"I'd rather you did."

"What about if I drive with the car windows open, and let my hair blow in the wind?"

"That's fine with me."

"And do I have to wear all that junk on my face all of the time, if I don't want to?"

"Only when you feel like it."

"Oh good," I said, starting to pull away from him. "I'm going to put on my favorite blouse and shorts right now."

Bob hugged me tighter.

"You mean the pink and blue blouse and the red shorts?" His voice broke.

"Umm hmm."

Bob was so excited to have the old me back. He just hugged and hugged. It seemed as though he was almost afraid to let me go.

Dentramental

"What do you mean, there's nobody to take our old dentist's place?"

"It's awfully hard to find somebody to fill our old dentist's shoes," I told Bob, giggling in a serious sort of way.

Bob laughed then, too. We had left our good old, tried and true, dentist behind when we moved to Minnesota, of course. We missed him.

"You mean to say, that of all the dentists here on the Iron Range, you haven't found one, not one, in all this time to call our own?"

"Nary a one," I said sadly.

"What about the one you took R.V.," (no that's not a misprint), "to, to get that extra tooth, that looked like a fang, removed? Wasn't he any good?"

"Naw. No sense of humor."

"Meaning?"

"Meaning that, when I told him we wanted that fang removed, because the boy acted strange when the moon was full, he didn't laugh."

Bob rolled his eyes. "Not everyone is like our old dentist," he reminded me.

Nope! Unique, that's what he was.

"Well now, how's my least favorite family?" our dentist would growl, in welcome.

"Whadda ya mean, 'least favorite?'" I would ask in mock anger.

"Not much money in you guys. Everybody in your family has good, healthy teeth. If it wasn't for the fact that you are all so clumsy, I'd get no money out of you, at all."

"Come on, now," I retorted, "I'm sure that there are other people who run into telephone poles."

"Not while they're walking," and he would guffaw and slap his knees.

We actually had a good relationship with him. Bob told him once, that he expected him to use his feet to pry open a patient's mouth.

"Nope," he said, "too dangerous. My feet are too tender to withstand being bit, and people tend to complain if I try that with my shoes on."

He was outspoken, bigoted, stubborn and cantankerous. He had some bad qualities, too.

Once in his chair, one was, of course, at his mercy.

He would lean way over, reach for an instrument, glower into his victims eyes if they were open, or yell, "What's the matter, you coward? Open those eyes!" if they were closed.

I never saw him without a cigarette in his mouth.

Scene: Patient lying back on chair, mouth open, eyes wide with terror. Big, white-coated doctor leaning forward, cigarette with long, long ash dangling precariously from lower lip.

Doc: So whadda ya think of those idiots in Washington?

Patient: Gaaraaw!

Doc: Boy, I think they should all be recalled. I never voted for any of them. How about you?

Patient: Gaaraaww!

Doc, leaning back and taking four drills, suction hoses and chisels out of patient's mouth: Did you ever imagine, in your life, that our country would be run by such a bunch of crazies?

Patient, nodding his head, shaking it vigorously, gulping for air: Uh, no, er, yes, uh. Boy ain't it somethin'.

Doc, leaning forward with all his paraphernalia back into the mouth, perpetual cigarette bobbing threateningly: Yeah, I know what you mean.

Fadeout.

"So how did it go at the new dentist's office?" Bob wanted to know.

"Eehh,"

"Didn't care for him, huh?"

"Well, Bob it's so hard to relate. I mean, here's this polite person, hanging over your face, being all serious, complaining, politely, because you haven't had anything done in a long time. Warning of dire problems ahead, but, lacking some sort of distinction. No political arrogance. No intimidation. No cigarette."

"No good?" Bob asked.

"No class."

Old Faithful

"That's a nice looking dog you've got there," a visitor mentioned.

I looked at Obediah. He certainly was a good-looking dog. I smiled.

"Is he a one man dog?" the visitor wanted to know. "Does he belong to Bob?"

"Well, no. He's part of the family, you see. But he does have a favorite, and it isn't Bob."

"Oh?"

I smiled again. "The dog is mine."

We had gotten him for our little guy, Micah. Micah was nearly three then and faster than a speeding bullet when it came to disappearing into the woods.

"Socrates," I would shout to our overworked, part St. Bernard. (Overworked meant that he had to roll over by himself, if the sun happened to be too warm).

"Socrates, where's Micah?"

I would wave my arm in the general direction of the woods and Socrates would struggle to his feet, shake his great head, throw a look of utter disgust my way and amble off into the forest; leading me straight to the fearless little boy who was busy "'sploring".

"Socrates has a great nose, and I think that everyone should have an eighty-five pound lapdog, but he just doesn't have the protective instincts that a German Shepherd has," I told Bob for the thousandth time.

"Umm hmmm," Bob said. "I can't afford a German Shepherd."

Determination is one of my best/worst qualities. I found one that we could afford.

"Now kids," I told the children, The people that own these puppies want someone who will love them and care for them, and so they are willing to sell us one for what we an afford."

They were excited.

"Now when Daddy comes home, we are going to be, oh, so nice, and butter him up, so that he will see what a good bargain this puppy is."

Subtle politicking, my forte.

Micah met Bob at the door.

"Hi, Dad. We're gonna butter you up for a shepherd puppy."

So much for subtlety.

We brought the puppy home, named him, taught him manners and obedience and gave him lots of love. He returned it all to us over and over.

But, he was my dog. He followed Micah into the woods, Rebekah on her bike, Sally and Leah to the mailbox or barn. He followed them, that is, if I told him to, "guard".

"I notice that Obediah never leaves your side," Bob mentioned one day. "I thought we got him to keep track of the kids."

"Yeah, I know," I moaned. "Today when we went walking, the children went down toward the river and I went the other way. They called and called him, but he wouldn't leave me. I guess he figures that they can take care of themselves, but I'm incompetent. Sigh."

Later, I began to think about the situation a little more. If I was in the living room, there sat Obediah. If I went up the stairs, so did Obediah. If I went outdoors to hang clothes, do chores, check mail, go for a walk, he was trotting along with me. At night, he made the rounds of everybody's room, but slept near my side of the bed. When I got up, he tagged along behind. If I overslept, he would come and howl in my ear. It was a compliment, I decided. He was one of those loyal, faithful to the death, kind of dog.

I was the one chosen to be worthy of his devotion. I was touched beyond measure.

We have an outdoor furnace room. When the weather is really super cold, we fire up the wood stove and stay cozy, toasty warm. Much, much warmer than with the other fuel.

It was super cold.

It was two o'clock in the morning.

"Bob," I hissed, "somebody needs to go stoke the outdoor furnace."

He ignored me, pretending to be asleep.

I tried a few more times and finally, facing reality, decided that if the fire was going to keep burning, I would have to do the stoking.

I put on my robe, slipped into my slippers, and thudded down the stairs.

Obediah followed.

I opened the back door, fighting the ferocious wind that grabbed at the door and nearly tore it from my grip.

"Come on, Obediah," I cried, "let's go."

My faithful friend looked out the door, turned his head to one side, to better hear the wind roaring past. He glanced, a loyal glance, at me.

He came to my side, leaned his faithful head against my knee, then turned smartly and ran up the stairs.

He was sound asleep when I finally got back into the house, and numbly climbed the stairs. He was also sleeping by Bob's side of the bed.

Some of My Best Friends Are

I have a friend who is a psychologist. The year before she got her degree, she introduced me to a fellow classmate of hers. I have often wondered, strange wonderings about this fellow classmate of hers.

As we shook hands, she gazed boldly into my face. This makes me nervous. I don't look at other people's faces and I sure don't like it when they stare into mine.

"I make you nervous, don't I?"

"Of course not," I lied. "Why do you say that?"

"Because you won't look directly at me."

"I rarely look directly at anyone," I explained, forcing myself to look directly at her.

"Why is that? Is it because you feel inferior to others?"

I whipped a glance to my friend. She was standing with her hands folded, her eyes closed, and a look of pious innocence wreathed her face.

I looked back at the budding psychoanalyst.

"I don't much care for faces," I said evilly, "I'm really into bodies."

Before the lady could respond, Carol, my friend, laughed out loud, grabbed my arm and guided me toward the parking lot.

"We had better get going," she said.

I was to drive them to their respective homes.

As we traveled down the expressway, we carried on a varied and lively conversation. Most of the lady's sentences started with... "Why do you say that?" "What makes you respond in that manner?" "Why do you feel that way?"

I began to feel as though she had tapped my head with a mental spigot and was slowly draining my brain away. It bothered me. I wasn't sure that I could afford the loss.

Suddenly, in the side mirror, I saw a police car pull up behind me. I sat up straight. Both hands gripped the steering wheel. I clamped my teeth together. He didn't drive around. He stayed there. Right behind. Making me tense. Uneasy.

"What's wrong?" Carol asked.

"Cop," I said. "Right behind me. I hate it when they follow me like that."

"You're doing the speed limit, aren't you?"

"That's not the point. I just don't like having them stay right behind me."

"Do you hate policemen?" The classmate again.

I thought of my dearest friend, Zip, and her husband, a born police officer. I didn't answer.

"Perhaps they remind you of your father."

That was one of the longest rides I had ever endured. My friend, Carol, mostly rode with her hand over her mouth. I couldn't decide if she was secretly laughing, trying to keep from talking or getting ready to be ill.

Several years later, while traveling across the country, I was reminded of that incident.

"Look Mom," one of the children shouted, "Highway 35, that way."

Quickly, I whipped the steering wheel and hove into the middle lane. We were fifteen minutes into Kansas City. It was almost five o'clock. I pretty well figured that we were doomed.

Bob had said that we might get separated in the traffic and instead of following him, I should just watch the highway signs. "Just stay on Highway 35", he had told me several times. "We'll meet on the other side of the city."

I thought he had said, "On that other shore," it made me even more nervous.

Of course, it never occurred to either of us to stop, and rest, and eat, and wait for the heavy traffic to subside, and then travel on through the city. No. We were there, we must keep going.

Apparently, someone had been studying the writings of Count de Sade. The signs had been positioned so that, as one drove merrily along, feeling comfortable in the "thru traffic," lane, suddenly, one was struck with a sign declaring… "I-35, right lane." "Quick!" Of course, the word, "quick," was not on the sign. It didn't need to be. Intimidation had already set in.

Later another sign would appear, "I-35, left lane, one/tenth of a mile." Then, "I-35, exit, back there!"

I tried to follow Bob and the moving van. Cars whipped around us, between us. I looked in the mirror.

Cop! Oh no! Just what I needed to add to my shattered nerves.

I sat up straight. Both hands gripped the steering wheel. I clenched my teeth. He didn't drive around us. Up ahead, Bob was suddenly changing lanes. What could I do? I flicked the turn signal. Cars whipped past. I couldn't move over. Couldn't change lanes. Then…

The police car behind me moved into the next lane. He didn't pass. He slowed the traffic, somewhat. Apparently, he had noticed the out of state plates on my vehicle. Seen that I was trying to follow the moving van. He was making room for me to change lanes. He stayed with us to the end of the heavy traffic. Helping us. Being there when we needed him.

Maybe Carol's classmate was right, after all. Sometimes the police officers do remind me of my father.

Florence Nightingale, I'm Not

Members of our household rarely become ill. It's not that we have some special, secret formula. The secret, if that is what one would call it, is that Mommy doesn't know how to behave around people who are ill.

Splinters, flu, loose teeth, cuts and bruises are all handled by Daddy, or if he isn't around, an older brother or sister. If absolutely no one else is available and it really can't wait, I will, through my own tears and my own cries of anguish, take the necessary steps to alleviate the suffering. My own suffering continues on for hours.

My friend, Jean, got her neck broken. Just hearing about it sent spasms of pain coursing through my body. Being a conscientious friend, however, I naturally went over to visit her.

She was sitting up with a horrible halo contraption skewered into her skull. She smiled. I thought I would faint.

"So what happened?" I asked cheerily. A little too loud, perhaps.

"Oh, it was the llama," she replied calmly. "He got frightened and I tried to hold onto him. He knocked me down."

Jean has a llama. She also raises sheep, black and white. She raises pedigreed dogs, too. In her spare time, she spins wool and knits. She is a very busy, accomplished woman. We have very little in common. Still, we are friends.

Later, as her injury began to heal, she called and asked if I would drive her to Duluth, to the doctor there.

"You mean in my car?" I asked.

"We can go in my van. I just need someone to drive for me. I can't turn my head, remember?"

"Oh, yes. Right."

My mind conjured up the vision of the halo. The screws drilled into her head. The metal bars going down across her shoulders. I began to feel faint again. "Wouldn't you be more comfortable in an ambulance?" I asked hopefully.

We arranged for me to pick her up on the appointed day. We decided to go in my car, after all. Much less stress on the driver, therefore on the passenger. I busied myself, mentally, for the trip.

I wonder, sometimes, if there is some parallel dimension to ours out there, where, just like in the movies, ominous music stirs off in the distance, and if we only paid attention, we could escape so many unpleasantries.

Like those people in the water in *JAWS*. There they are, swimming, playing, enjoying life…then…

THUM, THUM…THUM, THUM… but they don't hear. THUM, THUM, …they have been warned, but they continue on…THUM, THUM…gulp!

To keep Jean from hurrying out to the car after I got there, and possibly hurting herself, I decided to call her, and tell her that I was leaving my house. This would give her plenty of time to gather herself, and carefully get outside, safely. I called.

She was crying when she finally answered the phone. To answer the phone she had to descend the stairs. I hadn't thought of that. In doing so, she stumbled on a dog's toy and tumbled the rest of the way down.

"Are you hurt?" I nearly blasted her eardrum.

"I don't know. It does hurt."

"I'll be right there."

Instantly, I was out the door and into the car. I clicked on the hazard lights and roared out of the driveway. It's a good ten rural miles between our houses, but I saw no sign of another living being. I was hoping for a sheriff's car to flag down, because, quite frankly, I did not want to get to her place alone.

I pictured her lying there by the phone, gasping, all alone; and then I would come in begging her forgiveness. Naturally, she would forgive me. She's like that. Then, because there would be nothing anyone could do, I would kneel on the floor beside her and while she weakly grasped my arm, I would cool her fevered brow with my own cool, calm hand until the end.

By the time I pulled into the Cedarhurst gate I was sobbing so hard, I could barely see.

She met me at the door.

We had such a good time in the Big City, I volunteered to drive her there for her next appointment.

My car was in the repair shop when her next appointment time arrived. No problem, she assured me. I could drive her van.

I was hesitant. I had invited an eighty-year-old neighbor to accompany us, but that was when I thought that I would be driving my own car.

That was fine, Jean said. There was no reason to be hesitant. There would be plenty of room. Though I wasn't familiar with the vehicle, it had power steering and power brakes. What could possibly go wrong?

I should have been listening, off somewhere, in that other parallel dimension ...THUM, THUM...THUM, THUM.

Which Way Did it Go?

The pager started squawking just before midnight. I sat up in bed and listened carefully, as the disembodied voice intoned the fact that our volunteer fire department was needed at once. I registered the householder's name and road number in my half-awake brain. The voice gave other information, but I didn't register all of it, to my sorrow.

Leah, who has a penchant for neatness that she inherited from Bob, had hung my fire gear neatly and separately, on hooks in the back porch. It took me nearly ten minutes just to get the pants and boots back together properly, and to get them on my, still asleep, body. I put on the fire coat, and hat, and gloves as I hurried to the car.

The truck had already left the fire hall by the time I got there, so I drove off into the night, my eyes scanning the sky for the telltale glow that would guide me to the fire scene.

The only telltale glow that I could see was the moonlight glittering over the densely growing tree tops. I tried to recall the road numbers in our area. My recall didn't seem to be functioning. I returned to the fire hall and checked the maps. Aha! The householder's name and number corresponded, somewhat, to my own generalized memory of the area. Back in the car, I roared off to my destiny.

There was no fire. No truck. No cars. Nothing.

I must have the wrong fire number, I decided, and kept driving. The woods seemed to get denser and the road narrower. No homes or driveways were in evidence, anywhere. I turned down another road. The road was plowed but there were no driveways down there, either. The ice crystals sparkling on the trees and bushes, and on the road itself, seemed to declare that no one had driven down that way for a long, long time.

I stopped the car and rolled down the window, listening for the sound of people. There was nothing. It was quiet As they say, too quiet. Hastily, I rolled the window up and locked the doors. I drove on until I came to a break in the woods, where I could turn around. I drove back, lonely, dejected, a fireman all dressed up, and no where to go. A snowy owl whisked in front of me from the road side; the only other life I'd seen since I had left the house. I drove back to the fire hall. It was one-fifteen. No one was there. I went home.

Later I had found out that I had heard only part of the call. I had the right name, but the wrong area. Our department had been called to assist another department, several miles away. I didn't feel quite so bad.

Over coffee the next morning, I told Bob all about my adventure and explained that I had just one regret.

"What's that?" he wanted to know.

"Well, just think of the missed opportunity," I said. "If I could only have seen a highway patrolman. I could have flagged him down, and then swaggered over to his car, in all my fireman gear, and then when he rolled down his window, I could have leaned on the door, and looked in and smiled and said, 'Okay, buddy, where's the fire?'"

Horse Traders and Horse Sense

Bob was in for the surprise of his life. All alone, I had saved and saved, until I had saved enough money to buy a horse. A very special horse, for a very special man.

He had mentioned, once, that when he was a little boy, he had wanted, so terribly to own a horse. They were very poor and, of course, unable to afford so expensive a pet. Touched by this pathetic tale, I resolved to make his dream come true. I would buy my sweet husband a horse. A horse of his very own. His dream horse.

"Hello," I said into the phone, "do you have any registered Appaloosa stallions for sale?"

The owner of The Big Name Appaloosa Horse Ranch hesitated before answering.

"Are you sure you want a stud?" he asked.

"A what?"

"A stallion."

"Oh, yes, I'm very sure. See this is for my husband to ride and he just loves Appaloosas."

"But why a stallion?"

"Well, isn't a stallion a boy horse?"

A very hesitant, "Yes."

"Well then, of course, he would want a stallion. I read somewhere, that real men only ride stallions."

"John Wayne rides mares," he whispered.

"Really?"

We talked a little, and I was finally convinced that Bob would not die of absolute shame if he had a girl horse instead of a boy horse.

"Okay," I said cheerfully, "I'll take a registered mare. How much are they?"

"My mares start at six thousand five hundred dollars."

"Th, th, th, thousand dollars?" I said weakly. "Don't you have anything cheaper? I haven't got quite that much."

"Well, how much do you have to spend?"

"Three hundred dollars," I said in a very subdued voice.

The man was very polite, but we really didn't have too much to talk about after that. We hung up, cordially, but definitely.

I called my friend, Zip, who did her best to talk me out of, what she considered, the beginnings of a disaster. When she realized that she could not prevail on my good sense, she agreed to accompany me, as I made the rounds of all the, "Horses for sale," ads in the newspaper.

"Boy, I didn't know that common, ordinary, unregistered horses cost so much money," I whined to Zip.

"I still think that you're making a big mistake," she warned for about the twenty-seventh time.

We drove on, and on, and on. We stopped at all the places listed in the paper. Not one animal was in my price range. At last, with hope nearly gone, we began cruising down little side roads, dejectedly watching for some type of encouragement.

Suddenly, a sign ahead.

"HORSES 4 SALE." It was scrawled in pencil, across a piece of folded cardboard. The cardboard was nailed to a stick, and the stick was jammed crookedly, into the gooiest, stickiest, mud yard, I had ever seen.

"This is it!" I cried with delight. "I know that this is the place. I can feel it in my bones."

The car had barely rocked to a halt before I had jumped out and begun sloshing my way through the thick, gooey mud.

A real cowboy leaned across the top of a wooden rail fence. He chewed a toothpick, as he nonchalantly watched us make our way toward him.

"Hi," I said as we came stumbling up to the fence.

He nodded a greeting toward us.

"I see you have horses for sale."

"Yep."

We all stood there in silence, looking at one another.

"Well, I want to buy a horse."

"How much money you got?"

I hesitated; after all, I wasn't born yesterday.

"One hundred fifty dollars," I told him boldly.

He stood there for several long minutes, casually looking us over. Finally, he turned and, without a word, walked away toward an old tumbledown building. He disappeared around the corner.

Zip and I stood there, not knowing what to do. At last, he returned, leading a brownish colored horse.

"This here horse," he said, "costs one hundred and fifty dollars."

Zip gasped.

"I'll take it," I said, startling all three of us.

"Won't Bob be surprised?" I added to my dear friend.

She didn't say anything. She just put her head down on her arm, and her arm on the rail. It almost sounded as though she were crying. Happy to have found a horse at last, I guess.

A Horse Called Love

I had surprised my husband, Bob, with a horse, something he had always wanted. He was certainly surprised.

"Oh, Honey," he gasped when he first saw his brand new, very own horse, "you didn't pay money for that, did you?"

"Yes, I did," I told him proudly. "I picked her out all by myself, and did some fancy talking, too. I saved half the money that I had saved for the horse, for you to buy a saddle."

"How much?" he barely whispered.

"A hundred fifty dollars." I began to wring my hands. This was not quite the reaction that I had anticipated.

"That much?" He looked numb, almost faint.

"Don't you like her? I got her just for you. Because, you always wanted a horse. Because, I love you. Isn't it a good horse?" I started to cry.

"Oh, no, Honey, I love it. It's a good horse." He walked over to where his new horse stood.

She wasn't leaning against the fence anymore, as she had been doing, ever since the cowboy had ridden her all the way over from South Presa Street. A long and tiring, five miles, or so. It had clearly been an arduous trip for her. Now, she had her front hooves spread apart. Her knees pointed very definitely inward, almost touching each other. Her nose rested on the ground.

Bob patted her. "What a nice horse," he said jovially. "My, this is a good horse. Boy, what a great horse." His hand slid down her back into the nice deep hollow where the saddle would rest. "This is a horse. Oh boy, is this a horse. And it's mine. My very own horse."

By this time, he was, apparently, overcome with deep emotion. He dropped his head on his horses' back and sighed deeply. It almost seemed as though he were about to cry.

"Why don't you ride her?" I suggested. The children, who had been very quiet until now, agreed.

Bob lifted his head and looked at us blankly, for a few seconds. He sighed, and with a quick spring, leaped up, and slid gracefully onto her back.

"She's a very gentle horse," I told him, "She's had lots of babies, the man said, and he called her a brood mare. Isn't that sweet?"

Bob gazed down at me. His eyes began to glaze over. I decided that I had better tell him the bad part.

"She's not an Appaloosa," I said soberly.

"What?"

"No spots. I couldn't afford an Appaloosa."

Bob looked behind him, at the horse's rump.

"She is a Greenbroke though, whatever brand that is."

This time the look on his face was sheer amazement. Carefully, he slid to the ground. He sighed, a very deep sigh. He came over to where I stood. He spoke very carefully. Very gently.

"A green broke is not a breed," he said, "a green broke is a horse that is not trained. That bucks and kicks and tries to kill people when they try to ride."

"But, but, she let you get on her just now. She didn't do anything."

He sighed again, even more deeply. "That's because, whoever rode her out here, bucked her out, and probably wore her out. Her physical condition is not one of great stamina. Thank goodness."

"Couldn't you do that, though? Tame her, I mean?" I asked.

Bob looked at me. He didn't say anything. He just took my hand, and brought it to his mid-section.

"Oh. I forgot about your back brace. You probably would break your back again, if you got on a bucking horse so soon out of the hospital, and all. Right?"

"Something like that. And, Honey, because she's a brood mare, doesn't mean that she's sweet. It just means that she's had, er, babies. Lots of them, and she was probably rarely petted, and was mostly out on the range. Wild."

"Oh, I'm sorry." I felt pretty ignorant.

"It's okay." He hugged me and then laughed. "Now," he said, "what shall we feed my horse?"

"Oh, there's plenty of grass." I pointed to our little city lot.

"Not enough," he replied, smiling. "Besides, we can't keep her here. The neighbors may complain."

"Whatever for? She doesn't smell bad, does she? You have to, practically, be right on top of her, to smell her."

Bob kept smiling that same, stiff smile. He patted my shoulder.

"I'll go and see if I can find some hay. And, maybe a stable to rent for her." He hugged me again. "I've thought of a name for my horse."

"Really? What?"

"Love."

"Oh, Bob, you are so sweet. You know what? I'll betcha this day will totally change our lives."

He smiled. He was still smiling, as I watched him go out to the truck and climb inside. I don't know if he was still smiling while he was sitting, there banging his head over and over against the steering wheel.

Give Until It Hurts

The arrival of our family usually brought joyous palpitations to the heart of any pastor, when we entered a church. Our family, alone, would fill a whole pew. Warm bodies aside, we sang lustily and mostly remained awake during the sermon.

One particular Sunday morning, we were comfortably ensconced in our favorite pew. The halfway point, we had discovered, was the perfect spot to avoid being too noticeable. The people in the first rows are, of course, always in the forefront, so to speak. The people in the last rows are conspicuous, by reason of their desire to make a quick getaway. We preferred the nice, safe, nonentity of middle ground.

On this day, the hymns had been sung, the prayers made, announcements read and then more prayers, before the collection plates were passed around. Throughout the church, the sound of pocketbooks snapping and zipping and coins clinking and the soft swish of bills being pulled from wallets, betrayed the fact of minds on earthly lucre instead of heavenly blessings.

The taking of the collection is, of necessity, a solemn time. While some people wrestle with their conscience, others grit their teeth with determination, still others smile serenely. Those in charge of paying the church bills struggle to look unconcerned and confident. The soft, soothing organ music helps everyone.

Our family has had certain mandates for giving for, lo, these many years, so we had no inner struggles of how much to give. Nor were we on any boards or committees, so we had no cares as to how much others gave. A peaceful time for us.

The collection plate went across the first row, was passed to the second, then slowly, inexorably, it drew nearer and nearer to our row. Soon, Bob had the plate. He dropped in his offering and passed it to the child sitting next to him. The plate continued toward the middle of the pew where I sat, flanked by our two youngest. Then it was placed carefully into our youngest child's hands. I reached to help.

"I got it." The little one whispered, pulling away.

The sibling on my right reached around to help. I pushed her hand away. The collection plate teetered precariously. Four sets of hands dived for the rescue. Too late. It slipped. I slapped my hand up, under the plate, to keep it from falling more.

"Oh, no!" I gasped in a stage whisper.

A massive group intake of breath hissed around us as the plate surged upward. Helping hands appeared from all sides.

"I got it!" I yelled, as I executed a beautiful volleyball save with both hands.

The plate flew upward far above my head, it did a complete, graceful somersault in the air, broadcasting coins and bills and checks across a three row span.

"The pastor really didn't want to strangle me," I assured the children on the way home. "He was just joking. Right Bob? Bob?"

I guess he didn't hear me.

The Laws of Travel

"Now, we might get separated in heavy traffic, or some such. Do you think you can find your way to the campground? I'll mark it on the map for you."

"Of course, I can find it, Silly," I laughed. Anybody can follow a map. You don't have to mark it."

Bob looked at me dubiously. "I'll mark the map," he said.

I took the map, kissed him farewell and drove off. Confidence radiated from my wave as I dangled my hand from the window. Anybody could follow a map.

We were moving to Minnesota.

I drove our van. Bob was driving the big moving van and pulling a horse trailer behind. Everything was planned down to the simplest coffee break. We had worked it all out very carefully. This move would be uncomplicated and uneventful. After all, the trauma of pulling up stakes and moving to another part of the country, where we had no relatives and where the lifestyles were totally different, would be complicated and eventful enough.

A lot of people don't realize it, but there are two natural laws that Newton and those other guys never discovered.

The first is, that all traffic, within a twenty-mile radius of any large city, will instantly quadruple in size at precisely four-thirty-five, on any given weekday.

The second: No matter what time of day a person may begin a trip; they will reach the outskirts of every large city in their path, at precisely four-thirty-five.

Some cities have diabolical addendums to these laws. We were entering one such city.

The diabolical addendums? Under construction. Detour.

The first indication that the map I was using for a guide was worthless, came at four-thirty-three. A huge yellow and black striped sign with blinking orange-lighted arrows ordered us off the highway. Three million detour signs appeared to help me decide what to do next.

"One hundred thirty-third Street, this way!" "Downtown, this way!" "Lavish Manor Hills Road, this way!"

None of the names looked familiar from the map. I searched frantically for Bob and the moving van and horse trailer. Nowhere in sight, of course. I was on my own. Cars swarmed around me. I turned to the right and followed a station wagon piled with camping gear. I lost them.

Several hours later, with a van load of cranky children, one squawking parakeet and an unhappy dog, I drove into the campground. I was worried about poor

Bob trying to find his way through all that confusion. He was already there. Had been there for some time.

I had the tent. The camp stove. The food. He was not happy. We made a cold camp.

Next morning dawned bright and beautiful. We left at five-thirty. In consideration of our fellow campers, we did not eat breakfast there, but planned to meet at a nice highway restaurant some miles down the road. Bob left first. He failed to tell me that he would be stopping to get gas and oil.

All was well. Everyone was rested. There was, as yet, no morning rush-hour traffic. The map was functional again. We were on schedule.

The sign ahead said, “Breakfast with us at Nickerson Farms.”

“We’ll be caught up with Dad in just a few minutes, kids,” I declared.

Another sign hove into view. “Good breakfasts at the Red Barn.”

Oh, no.

Farm? Barn? Which one? I couldn’t remember. Bob hadn’t marked that part on the map. Both names conjured up the same vision in my mind.

As we neared the first restaurant, I slowed and ordered the children to look for their father. After all, a moving van and horse trailer would be pretty conspicuous.

He wasn’t there. Confidently, I speeded up and pulled into the second restaurant several miles down the road. Bob wasn’t there, either.

What now? With some irritation, I headed on down the highway. Obviously, Bob had forgotten that we were to stop for breakfast and had just kept traveling. Surely, we would catch up to him. With the moving van and horse trailer, he couldn't travel very fast.

Another ten miles and I was beginning to get nervous. I finally took a crossover and headed back.

"We'll go to the first restaurant," I told the children, "and start from there."

As we went whipping past restaurant number two, the children all cried out, "There's Dad! He's standing by the truck in the parking lot."

There was nothing that I could do. The next crossover was five miles away.

Bob, of course, had seen us go by. He had been champing at the bit, trying to stay unruffled, wondering why we were so late getting to the restaurant. After all, he reasoned, he had taken plenty of time, filling up the gas tank in the moving van and checking tires and all those necessities. Now, here we were, rushing by, heading in the wrong direction.

"What now?" he grumbled. He jumped into his vehicle and followed us.

At the next crossover, I pulled around quickly and headed back, post-haste, to restaurant number two.

We passed each other on opposite sides of the highway.

"Are you mad at me?" I asked Bob sometime later, as we all were sitting around, eating brunch.

"We may never see each other again," he said ominously.

"What? Why?"

"We're behind schedule. The next large city is Kansas City. We should get there around four-thirty."

What Whahr?

"Darlinka," my friend from Poland greeted on the phone, "how do you spell 'dawble'?"

"What?"

"Dawble."

"Dawble?" I said, playing for time. What did she mean by, "Dawble?"

"You know what I'm saying? Like two things."

"Oh, yes," I said, seeing the light. "Dawble. D-o-u-b-l-e. dawble."

I admire anyone who can speak more than one language. Even if they sometimes get the sounds a bit confused. Maybe the word is not, admire. Maybe it's envy.

My inabilities, when it comes to speaking a foreign language, are phenomenal. Though I am able to translate in my mind, it never quite sounds right going past the lips. Grown men shudder whenever I try to utter a pronouncement in a foreign language.

My English ain't so good, neither.

Once, after a string of my misspoken utterances, Bob could endure no more.

"Honey," he said, "you sure do pernounce them words purty."

Accents, though, are really my downfall. I pick up on the sound of the accents wherever I happen to be living for awhile, and carry it with me when I leave.

When we lived in Newfoundland; why, Newfoundlanders thought that I was one of their own. When we lived in Tennessee, Alabama and Texas, why, ya'll couldn't tell me apart from a real Southerner. Omaha? "You'se guys catch on?" Of course, I had no idea that I sounded strange to anyone. It sounded right to me.

The first spring that we were on the Iron Range of Northern Minnesota, I took a trip into town with R.V., (not a misprint), one of our older boys. We went to the feed store.

"What can I help you with, today?" The man wanted to know.

"Yes," I said pleasantly, "I need some whahr."

"Some what?" he asked pleasantly.

"Some whahr."

The man looked at me blankly.

"For my chikins," I added helpfully, pleasantly.

The man's brow wrinkled in concentration. "Again?" he said.

Now I began to feel like an alien. Frustrated, the heavy, Deep South, drawl from my youth, slipped into play.

"Whahr," I said, "Ah need sum chikin whahr."

The man leaned forward. Earnestly trying to decipher. To translate. We were both trying too hard.

"What are you going to do with it?" he asked.

"Put mah chikins in it, of course."

A look of understanding swept over his face.

"A water fountain for your chickens!" he exclaimed.

I stared at him. Dumbfounded.

"No," he muttered to himself, "that's not it."

R.V., (not a misprint), who had been going to school amongst the native Iron Rangers, and was, therefore, bilingual, was chuckling up his sleeve.

"Mom," he said gently, "that's wiyer."

"Huh?"

He turned to the man. "She wants to buy some rolls of chicken wire."

"Oh, chicken wire." The man looked very happy.

Later that day, one of the neighbors called.

"You busy?"

"We're fixin' to put up a fence."

"You mean you're repairing a fence?"

"No. We're just now fixin' to put it up. It's brand new." Then I added, just to show I could speak her language, "It's wiyer."

"It's what?"

"It's wiyer."

She was silent for a minute, then, "You guys sure do talk funny."

Pure Panic

The corn stalks crackled ominously as my fellow teenage friend led the way through the Nebraska fields, following the shortcut to her house.

Of course, the subject of wild animals and dead bodies came up, and we discussed these subjects in an extensive, mature, and knowledgeable manner, even though we knew very little about them.

"If I ever ran into a wild animal," I assured her, "I would stand my ground and stare it right in the eye and make it back away from me. That's what you do, you know. It makes them confused."

"I know," she said, solemnly, "but, we'll have to be brave and help each other."

We then continued on, though we traveled a little more slowly. Looking carefully to either side, then peering cautiously ahead before taking a step, slows the progress, somewhat.

A slight rattling off to my left caused me to come to a full stop in mid-stride. My friend hadn't heard anything, apparently. She was getting a little too far ahead. My heart began thumping wildly. I wanted to stay behind to make sure nothing was creeping up on us from the rear, and yet I didn't want to be left there alone. I glanced around one more time. Then my friend screamed.

She screamed two more times. Deep guttural screams that pierced the air with terror and fear.

I caught sight of her face, as she rushed back toward me. Her eyes were wide with panic, her hands outstretched, she shoved me sideways and I tripped and fell into the cornrow. Then everything went blank.

Suddenly I was standing on the outer edge of the cornfield, watching my friend come racing toward me, frantically trying to get out of the cornfield herself. I wondered how she managed to still be in the field while I had already escaped. She looked very odd, I noticed. Her face was caked with dirt and her hair was all disheveled.

"What happened?" I queried.

"A humongous spider," she gasped, "all red and black! It was as big as my hand and in a web right across the path."

"A spider?" I said, "you were that scared of a spider?"

"Yes," she started to giggle, "I was terrified, but you should have seen you."

"Me? What did I do?"

"What did you do? Why," she said, "brave you, came thundering after me, and when I looked back, you were right behind me. Your mouth was hanging open and your eyes were great, big, and round, and staring straight ahead." She laughed again.

"I don't remember anything that happened," I told her, truthfully.

"Well," she continued, "I tripped and fell, and you ran right over the top of me. One foot on my bottom end and the other on the back of my head. You probably got out here in two more steps. I never saw such speed. Some brave friend you turned out to be."

I laughed sheepishly. "Well, you can rest assured that I really had your safety and welfare at heart."

"Oh, you did?"

"Sure. If what frightened you had been something really dangerous, I would have stayed to help you. Since it was just a spider, well, what can I say? There was no sense hanging around waiting for you to collapse with a heart attack or something. I wanted to get out of your way and rush into town for help if need be."

"Oh," she apologized, "I'm sorry that I doubted you." She sounded as sincere as I.

You Can't Get There From Here

"Did you bring the map?" Sharon asked.

"No, I forgot it, but don't worry. I looked at it very carefully. I've practically got a photographic memory, you know."

Sharon and Martha glanced at me. They obviously didn't believe me.

"Don't worry," I reassured them. "Nobody can get lost traveling between Hibbing and the Cities. You just go straight south."

"True," Sharon agreed, "I suppose, even you, won't be able to get lost." She didn't sound particularly confident.

The morning was clear. It wasn't quite six o'clock and the little Girl Scouts had quieted down in the back of the van.

"Boy, that sun sure is bright," Martha said.

"It sure is," we agreed, squinting and shading our eyes.

We traveled along, commenting now and again about how bright the sun seemed; especially since it was glaring straight into the windshield. It was thirty minutes before anyone questioned the position of the sun.

"Say, if we're going straight south, why is the sun directly in our eyes?"

We all agreed that it was a legitimate question.

"Now girls," I raised my voice to lecture the scouts in the back, "learn from this experience. If the sun is in your eyes in the morning, you're going east. If it's evening, you are going west." Warming to the subject, I added loftily, "We want to go south, so we must turn."

"Which way do we turn?" one of the girls wanted to know.

"Which way? Why, uh, er, why we turn to the, uh, to the…"

"South," Martha stated.

Eventually, we did find the Twin Cities.

Much later, Martha, having grown complacent with time, rode with me to a speech meet with some of the students from our school. It was being held in Anoka, a city near Minneapolis.

"Did you bring the map?" she asked.

"No, I forgot it. But, don't worry. I looked at it carefully and…"

"I know. You have a photographic memory." She sighed. "I hope we get there."

"There is no way that I can get lost this time," I told her. "We go straight down I-35 until we get to Highway 292, then we turn west. Simple."

"Okay," she said. Her voice did not sound too confident.

Many hours later, Martha began to question my photographic memory. "Funny," she said, "I thought Anoka was north of the Cities."

"Well, keep looking for Highway 292. It has to be around here somewhere."

"Are you sure that there is a Highway 292?" she asked.

"Somewhere in the world there has to be a Highway 292," I said.

"Apparently it doesn't go into Anoka," she replied, darkly.

She was right, and although we didn't quite get as far as the Iowa border, there was a lot of grumbling in the car before we reached our destination.

My experience at memorizing maps grew, along with a totally unjust reputation. I always managed to get where I was going, somehow. To downtown Minneapolis, by way of Edina. (Bob got especially testy and, let's face it, really grumpy, about that one). To Shakopee, by way of St. Paul. I got lost in Cook twice, (population 899), but that wasn't my fault. There was no map.

Then: A trip to North Dakota. Friends and neighbors solemnly patted Barbara's shoulder. "So, you're going out of state with Darlene driving." They would press their lips into tight little lines and shake their heads. "Well," they would say, but they didn't add to their statement.

Barb would assure them that she would be holding the map. It didn't seem to matter.

Obviously intimidated by the attitude of nearly everyone she spoke to, it began to tell on her nerves.

By the time our departure found us on the road heading west, she was gripping the map nervously.

"Don't worry," I told her, "I looked at the map carefully, I've got it memorized."

"Good," she said weakly.

"We'll go west on Highway 200 to Highway 34. Right?"

She looked at the map. "Right!" she said, surprised. "That's right."

"Now, don't panic, Barb, but we are going to take a little shortcut. State Highway 290. It'll save us a few miles. It's on the map. Don't worry."

I glanced at her. She looked worried. She studied the map. Apparently, she saw that I knew, indeed, what I was talking about, this time. She relaxed, visibly.

"People get bad reputations about something, sometimes, when it isn't their fault. Sometimes evil reputations are not even true. Now, you can see that I really have memorized that map. There is no way that I can get lost this time."

We drove along, confidently.

"Look. There's State Highway 290," I pointed out to her. I signaled, slowed and turned left, the only way we could turn. We saw a sign that said that we were, indeed, on state Highway 290. No mistakes for me. No siree. Not this time.

A pretty little shortcut, Highway 290 seemed to be a little different than the average state highway. Just ahead, we saw people strolling back and forth across the roadway. We drove slowly past a beautiful brick building on our right. On our left was a rather large parking lot. People waved to us in a friendly way and smiled. We smiled and waved back. Then we came to a field full of flowers. People were strolling in the field full of flowers. They were picking the flowers. They smiled and waved to us. What struck us as unusual about this particular field full of flowers, was that it was growing right across the highway.

We sat there. Staring.

"You did it again, didn't you?" Barbara asked, softly.

I nodded, too stunned to move or speak. We sat there for sometime. Finally, I took the map and studied it very, very carefully.

"Oh no," I groaned. "Look! Highway 290 is here all right, but if you look very, very closely, you can see that it doesn't go all the way through to the other highway. It doesn't go anywhere. It just stops. Here."

We looked up. Just ahead, on the other side of this beautiful flower filled field, we could see cars traveling; going past us. We studied the map once more.

"You practically need a magnifying glass to see that it's a dead end, though." I paused and looked, unseeing, through the windshield, trying to correlate what had happened. Finally, I understood. It was perfectly clear. This was a conspiracy. I began to babble.

"They did it on purpose. They knew, somehow, that I would eventually be going to North Dakota and they put this road here on purpose."

"Now, now, don't get upset." Barb soothed. "It could have happened to anyone." She stared at the map, "It's easier to see, now that I know what to look for. It does look like the highway goes right on through here, but looking really carefully at the map; you can see that it stops just short of connecting to the other highway."

"They did it just to trick me," I said, paranoia leaking out through all my pores.

"No, no. It wasn't a trick. Just turn around now and go back to Highway 200. Everything is just fine."

"They did it on purpose, though. They wanted to ruin my reputation, permanently. They want people to not trust me."

"Well, it didn't work," Barb said loyally. "I trust you and your ability just fine."

"Do you, really?"

"Yes, I do."

That made me feel better. Soon we were off, once again trying to find North Dakota.

"I appreciate the fact that you haven't lost confidence in me, Barb," I told her as we drove along. "It sure helps. Thanks."

"Don't mention it," Barb laughed, "but if it's all the same to you; next time I go anywhere, I'll have my husband do the driving."

Peppermint Shoe Polish

"They have a new kind of shoe polish out now," a friend informed me.

"Oh, really? What kind is that?"

"Peppermint flavored. So that it won't taste so bad the next time you put your foot in your mouth."

It's too bad that I didn't catch that brand name. I certainly needed something like that way back in my younger years, when I was working at the bakery.

I enjoyed working in a factory, especially the more menial tasks. That left my mind and body free to go their separate ways. I could do the routine work with my hands, while my mind was off in some Never, Never Land, enjoying unreality. I would be, as Bob would say, "Off in the land of Ambrosia," or if there was a friendly worker around, I could yak all day long, while I did the work, and still get paid. Either way, it suited me just fine.

There was only one blight on this situation. A woman, who resented the fact that I was. She would break into my day with cutting remarks that would reduce me to tears, even before we punched in at the time clock.

Bob and I discussed this an awful lot and he would try to encourage me with trite little sayings. "Just ignore her." Impossible. "She's hurting herself more than she's hurting you." I didn't buy that one either. We finally came up with a grand idea. I would return kindness for nastiness. No matter what she did, I would smile and say something nice to her, or preferably, something nice about her. I like challenges. Grimly, I looked forward to the next working day.

"Good morning," I beamed cheerily, as I entered the dressing room.

"Good morning." "Hi." "Hello." Lots of feedback from the other women. Nothing from, you know who.

I proceeded to change into my uniform when SHE came up to me. "Wouldn't you be more comfortable in a larger uniform? One that was your size?"

"Uh, er, duh," I replied.

By the time I had formulated something intelligent to say, like, "No," she had walked jauntily away.

At brake time, I would say something nice to her, I decided. I would think carefully until I formed an honest compliment to her. That would break through her reserve and we would become fast friends forever.

Unfortunately, my mind didn't have a chance to form any thoughts. We were assigned to an assembly line together. Right next to each other. "Think fast," I told myself. An improbable feat under perfect conditions. I listened in mounting horror, as she began her tirade against me.

"Think good thoughts," I ordered my mind. "Think something nice." I forced myself to look at her. "Say something complimentary," I ordered myself again. No use. This was too much of a challenge. I wasn't going to be able to make it work. Then suddenly, I realized that this woman looked just like a girl that I had met at a party years before. My hands flew along the cookie line, sorting and boxing while my mind whirled back to the party. Why, even their voices were very similar.

The grand idea was going to work, after all. I would tell her that she reminded me of a teenager that I had met years before. Tell her that she even looked like her. What a compliment. This woman was going to become my friend, or I was going to die trying.

"You know, you look just like a teenage girl I used to know," I cut into her venomous monologue. I was smiling just as sweetly as I could.

"Really?" She actually looked pleased.

"Yes," I replied, my mind skipping along. Bob was going to be so proud of me.

"You're just like her."

"Oh, really?"

"Yes," I said with genuine enthusiasm. "And I didn't like her either."

The Guardian

When I was sixteen, my dad was stationed at a SAC base near a very large city. We had been stationed out of the country for many years and this would be my first experience in a large, several thousand-student-body, high school.

Physical education was, of course, a required subject. I have never figured out why. We played team sports and, throughout the year, some girls sat on the benches and never moved a muscle. It was incomprehensible to me.

We also had lectures about our bodies, and what not to do to them; modesty, being the key word to all these lectures. Then, we were required to disrobe and shower in front of dozens of other girls. I didn't then, and I still don't understand the reasoning behind these seemingly opposite teachings.

I accepted the modesty teaching, since it went along pretty well with what my own mother had taught me, and simply refused to shower at school. This caused me uncounted grief in the form of detention and pages and pages of written, "I will obey" lines.

Volleyball was a new game to me. It looked like fun. Perhaps because I was new in gym class, I was chosen to be on a team. Volleyball was a little more complicated to play than I had anticipated. Out team lost. My fault.

Downstairs, in the dressing room, I was just finishing my discrete sponge bath, when someone smashed me into the locker door. Stunned, I turned to see five girls who had been on the team, forming a semi-circle around me. I glanced frantically over their heads. All the other girls were scurrying, some of them half-dressed, out of the room. There were gangs in the school, of course. Mostly divided by ethnic background. I had been told that some of the girl gangs were really mean. That the guy gangs were even afraid of them. Looking at this group, I found no doubt in my heart that I had just met up with one such gang. I heard a knife flick open. I instinctively knew that it was a knife. I didn't see it.

"I don't like to lose," the leader of the gang snarled.

I tried frantically to think of something tough and clever to say, like, "Hah! You were a born loser."

As I say, I tried to think of something, but even the, "Hah!" part didn't come to mind.

The girls began to call me names and to describe what would happen if I ever caused them to lose again. They were going to give me a sample, they said, so I would remember.

My mind whirled to some plan of action. Some way to save myself. What to do? What to do? John

Wayne had never been caught modestly clutching his blouse together, while five very angry girls threatened his face. Ditto the Lone Ranger. Even Wonder Woman had never been in a situation like this. I had no precedent to follow.

I would have to make my own decisive, imaginative escape.

Help! I tried to shout. That was the only decisive, imaginative plan that I could think up.

All five girls lunged to stop my mouth, but it wasn't really necessary. I was too terrified to make a sound. Inside, I was courageously screaming. Outside, I was quivering and shaking so hard that they could barely grab my arms.

"Back off!" a gravely female voice from another part of the room ordered.

Everybody moved back.

A big girl, about my age, came striding forward. She stood with her hands on her hips. She pretty nearly covered the whole locker area.

She looked at me. "You the one that lost the volleyball game?"

Fortunately, it was not a question that required an extensive reply. Since my head was already shaking, it was just a matter of forcing it to move up and down. I nodded.

"Nobody likes to lose," she said almost conversationally. "I don't like to lose." She looked at the other girls. "You don't like to lose." She nodded toward me. "Even she don't like to lose."

She stepped closer to me.

"You new here?"

Again, I nodded my head.

"You ever play volleyball before?"

I shook my head.

"You got two weeks. Nobody'll hurt you for two weeks. Hear?"

I nodded my head.

"My name's Irene. Nobody messes with Irene. Right?" She glowered at the other girls, obviously a rival gang, but not too rival. They were all, I noticed, nodding and shaking their heads. Like me.

A few days later, I managed to get myself trapped in an empty hallway with two tough looking girls demanding my wallet. Frantically, I barged into an untended history classroom. They came charging right behind me. There stood Irene, checking out the upcoming history test.

She glanced up.

"You in trouble again?"

Relief flooded over me.

"Not me. At least, I don't think so." I glanced at the two girls who were standing just inside the doorway.

"My friend, Irene wants to know if I'm in trouble." I said with a somewhat gloating swagger. I paused significantly, "Am I?"

It was a good year. I learned to sew. I met Bob. I got my first real, after school, job. I learned to play volleyball. I learned that guardian angels come in different colors and sizes.

Sightseeing With My Mother-in-law, Poor Thing

"We had quite an interesting day, Son," my mother-in-law said.

"Oh? Darlene take you sightseeing?" my husband inquired.

"Uh, it's almost time to eat," I interrupted. "The meat is nearly thawed."

Bob looked at me suspiciously. "What did you do to my mother?"

"We just went places," I laughed. "You know. Here and there. Ha, ha."

"Oh?"

"See, I took this other road," I explained quickly, "and we went around some very pretty territory. Right, Ma?"

"Right," she said. "We kept driving and driving. Rebekah wondered if we were lost. I told her not to worry. As long as we could see electric lines, we were fine."

"And then the electric lines disappeared," interrupted Rebekah.

"Yeah, and then I said I was starving to death," Micah's two cents worth.

"And Rebekah sighed and said she knew we should have brought provisions," my mother-in-law concluded.

"I got us back home, didn't I?" I justified. "Besides, there was no reason to panic. Even on the way out here we cover several miles without electric lines."

"Where did you go?" Bob wanted to know.

"Well," I fidgeted, "we drove around quite a bit."

"Where did you go?"

"Well, we sort of wound up in Big Fork."

"Big Fork? What were you doing way out there?"

"Trying to find Hibbing?" I said uncertainly, wringing my hands.

"Trying to find Hibbing? Where were you?"

"We were coming back from Grand Rapids."

"How could anyone wind up in Big Fork, going to Hibbing from Grand Rapids?" Bob demanded, unreasonably.

"Well, for one, just listen to what you just said," I reasoned, reasonably. "You just named three different towns. That's confusing. Then if one doesn't know exactly where the towns are located on the map, it gets more confusing."

"Did you have a map?" he asked.

"Of course not. Why would I need a map? For pity sakes, I've lived in this area for years."

Bob's eyes glazed over, which is the way he always ends these rather heated discussions, when he runs out of logic.

We proceeded on with the preparations for supper.

"So, what's on the agenda for tomorrow?"

"How about berry picking?"

"Please," Bob said in alarm, "don't take my mother into the woods. You get lost just going from the house to the barn when you take the short cut through that little patch of woods out here."

"That's not true," I declared, with some little warmth.

"Mom, how about the time when we were hiking behind the barn and you got us lost, and kept telling us not to panic. That Daddy and the boys and Socrates would find us by morning." Rebekah again.

"We got out, didn't we?"

"Sure," my child agreed, "But I'm the one that led us out."

"Maybe we could do some other type of activity," my mother-in-law interjected, "like embroidery."

"How about this?" I said, with a glower at everyone. "We can go canoeing. That would be fun. And, there's no need to worry. How could I get lost on the river?"

"That's true," everyone mumbled nervously.

"We live in a unique area," I told my mother-in-law the next day. "We can choose to canoe rivers that flow to the north, or we can choose to canoe on rivers that flow to the south. There are even some pretty steep falls to portage around and some rapids, in places, on some of these rivers."

"Are you sure you know which river is which?" she asked.

"Sure," I reassured, "after all, I've lived in this area for quite some time, you know."

Ordeal by Canoe

My mother-in-law is pretty easy going. She is somewhat adventurous, which is helpful when she comes to visit.

"Well, Ma," I asked, "ready to go in the canoe with me?"

She closed her eyes for a moment, praying, I suppose, and indicated that she was, indeed, ready.

We had decided to explore the river.

"Lakes are nice," I told her, "but rivers don't have those great, big spiders."

"Spiders?"

I told her about how Bob and I like to go fishing, and one anniversary we had gone, all alone, by ourselves, to a quiet little lake north of us, and had decided to explore an interesting island.

We had paddled smoothly through the rice that surrounded the island and neared the shore.

Suddenly, I had looked into the heavy vegetation where we were heading. Shriek! Scream! Hundreds of millions of giant spiders, with glowing eyes and huge fangs, were ready to leap upon us and devour us. With lightning speed, my mind devised a plan of escape. I jumped from the canoe and raced across the top of the water in two steps and landed, panting and palpitating, on the safety of the island.

"And left my poor son behind?" my mother-in-law accused.

"He's not afraid of spiders," I justified.

She eyed me speculatively, but didn't say anything.

"Okay Ma," I ordered when we reached our launch destination, "you get in first and I'll shove us off and hop in back, here."

Being a trusting soul, she did what I told her. She got into the front, picked up the paddle, faced forward, gritted her teeth and shouted that she was ready. Her voice quavered just a bit.

Surprisingly, I got us launched without incident, and we headed upriver.

"Why are we going against the current?"

"Lots of reasons," I assured her. "One is that we are fresh and strong, so paddling upriver is easier now than coming back, when we'll be tired."

"Oh, what's another reason?"

"Another reason, well to be truthful, another reason is that I don't like surprises, and going downriver, we might run into some rapids, or such, that we can't handle."

"That makes sense," she commented.

I was glad that she didn't ask anymore questions. I didn't want to tell her that I had no idea what we would run into going upriver, either, since I had never canoed this river before.

We would be able to handle it, though. I was sure.

We paddled along, enjoying the quiet scenery: the lovely blue sky, the sharp green of the trees, the yucky, brownish-red of the water, the yellow flowers along the bank.

"This is beautiful," my mother-in-law whispered, as she brushed aside a low hanging tree branch.

"It is," I agreed, as I brushed aside a few dozen mosquitoes.

"I've never experienced anything like this," she said as she slapped at a biting fly and pushed another low hanging branch away from her face.

"I love the out-of-doors," I exclaimed through gritted teeth, as I twisted my head around to locate the sound of the rustling on the shore, and missed seeing the tree branch. My glasses clunked to the bottom of the canoe.

"My, the river bank is certainly getting closer to us isn't it," she said nervously.

"Yeah," I answered, "we'll have to careful not to run aground."

"What will happen if we run aground?" she asked as the canoe came to a soft, crunching, jolting halt.

"One of us gets out to push," I sighed.

First, we tried to push off with the paddles, but that was not to be, oh no. Someone would have to get out onto the mud bar and push. Somehow, I knew that it would be me.

I eased myself gingerly over the side and sank past the tops of my shoes into the slimy, yucky mud. I tried to pull my feet free and sank past my ankles.

"If I live through this," I thought to myself, "I'm not going to do this anymore."

"Darlene!" my mother-in-law shouted. "What's that noise on the bank?"

I froze. Something was coming to get us. We could hear it crashing through the underbrush.

I pulled at my feet and shoved at the canoe. The sound of the creature was coming closer. I couldn't move my feet. They were stuck fast and sinking deeper. Nothing could be worse, I thought. Then I looked down at the water. Leeches!

"I've never seen anyone come down a river in a canoe sideways, before," several people commented a few minutes later, as we pulled up to our landing place. "And so fast, too," they added.

My mother-in-law looked down at my feet. A question was forming on her lips.

"Those were old shoes," I said nonchalantly. "I wanted to leave them behind."

Fair Is Fair

"Excuse me," I tapped the man on his arm, he turned, and I smiled brightly. "Have you seen my daughter and her friends?"

I suppose the fact that we were standing in front of the youth building on the state fairgrounds surrounded by thousands of young people, caused him to hesitate before he answered.

"Your daughter?" he asked politely.

"Yes. Remember me? You sat at the same table with our group at breakfast yesterday morning. She came by in her pretty dress that she had made."

This in-depth revelation of Rebekah's presence caused the poor man to very nearly reel in confusion. He glanced at my lapel and obviously recognized the pin that identified me as a bona fide chaperone for our organization.

"Er, well. Let's see. What was she wearing, today?" he asked.

"Blue jeans and a blue jean jacket," I said.

We both glanced at my blue jeans and blue jean jacket. Then at the lady walking past in her blue jeans and blue jean jacket. Then at the group of seven or eight youngsters, all crossing the street, in their blue jeans and blue jean jackets. Then at the forty-two blue jeans and blue jean jackets, bobbing along the sidewalk across the street, and at the five thousand, three hundred eleven blue jean jackets, weaving in and out of the crowd around us.

"She has longish brown hair," I added, hopefully.

"Uh, no," he said, "I don't believe I noticed her going by just now."

"We were supposed to meet here, but I got lost getting here from supper, so I'm a bit late," I explained. "We were going to the coliseum together."

"Oh, what's going on at the coliseum?"

"English horse show."

"Oh."

"You're not going there?" I asked, hopefully.

"No, that's not my cup of tea," he punned.

I smiled anyway.

"Well, if you see her, would you please tell her that I will meet them there?"

"Sure," he said.

I hurried along across the street and turned right, then corrected to some degree and was surprised to hear a marching band. A parade. I turned around and followed the music.

Slowly, I began to realize that people had stopped and were now gawking up at the sky. I stopped and gawked, mouth open, and gasped. A man was walking a high wire across the fairgrounds. Since I am not interested in watching people risk their lives to entertain me, I turned quickly, and clumped into the man from the youth building.

"I thought you were going to the coliseum," he said brushing the splashed pop from his jacket.

It seems as though I had been going the wrong way. He pointed me in the right direction and off I trotted. Fifteen minutes later, after passing the Milk House for the third time, I knew that I was lost, once again.

"Did you change your mind?" a weary voice queried.

Guess who.

"Well," I said looking around forlornly, "are you sure you don't want to go to an English horse show?"

Rebekah and her friends were already there, effusive in their comments on the gallantry of this kind stranger. He, having, by now, no confidence in my directional abilities, offered to stay and escort us all back to the dorms after the show.

I'm pretty sure the man had a miserable evening. It really didn't seem to be his cup of tea; though he didn't actually snore. I decided to try and cheer him up some.

"You are a very nice person," I assured him as we all trooped back to the dorms.

"Um," he said glumly.

"I mean, you gave up your whole evening just for us. Strangers. Now, that's pretty nice."

"Uhm, hmm," he answered.

"This has been a great fair," I said cheerfully.

"Uhm."

"Even the food's been good."

"Uhm."

"Our group leaves tomorrow, on a relatively early bus."

"Really?" he said, and smiled.

Is This The Better, Or Is This The Worse?

"Will you wear those gifts I bought you?"

"I certainly will," I assured the slightly befuddled neighbor lady.

"And, will you wear both gifts at the same time, please? They match each other so well."

"I, uh, er, of course," I said, wondering about that last statement.

The, very much past-retirement-lady was so very excited about my forthcoming wedding. She had watched every step of my mother's sewing as we worked on my wedding gown, and each day brought her to our house, almost as bubbly with excitement as I.

She had bought me two gifts to wear on that great day. A pair of glitzy earrings and, uh, an undergarment to match.

The wedding day arrived right on schedule. The neighbor lady called from the hospital. Her husband had been taken in, by ambulance, the night before. She would not be at the wedding. She would not get to see the bride, all beautiful, wearing those lovely gifts. There would be pictures, of course, but it would not be the same. There was only one statement for me to make, naturally, so I made it. Bob and I would come by the hospital after the wedding, in all our finery, just for her. She was very pleased.

The ceremony went fairly smoothly. The bridesmaid tumbled, face forward, down the stairs in front of the alter. She didn't get hurt. Later, a close friend knocked down three other women in her unsuccessful endeavor to catch the bouquet. No one was injured then, either. All in all, a day to remember.

After the reception, Bob and I drove to the hospital, sneaked in the back door, and made our way to the floor where the neighbor man was recuperating.

"Oh, you really did come to see us," the lady cried happily. "And you look so beautiful." She grabbed my hand and pulled me out into the hallway.

"Come look at the bride!" she shouted. "Come look at the beautiful bride."

Nurses and patients and other visitors peeped around corners and doorways. Some came up and shook hands and wished us happiness, etc. We didn't know what to do, so we just stood there smiling and shaking hands and saying thank you's.

"Isn't she beautiful?" the lady kept saying to all and sundry. "Her mother made that dress. Isn't it beautiful? And I bought her those earrings. Aren't they beautiful?"

I turned to her in alarm. Surely she wouldn't.

"Are you wearing those beautiful panties that I bought you?" she asked loudly.

I nodded, horrified.

"Look," she declared, and before I could back away, she grabbed my dress and lifted it nearly over my head; revealing under the beautiful wedding gown, the beautiful panties, that matched the beautiful earrings, that she had bought.

Later, as quickly as we could, Bob, crimson faced, and I, matching in complexion, managed to escape to the car and drive off.

"How could something like that happen?" Bob asked, musing. "I mean, that isn't normal."

"Well it isn't my fault," I declared defensively.

"No," he said slowly, eyeing me sideways, "but there is something about you that draws odd, strange, peculiar and unusual happenings."

I wondered if he were getting second thoughts about this marriage business, already.

"It's just one of those, once-in-a-lifetime experiences," I assured him. "Don't worry. There's not much else that can go wrong now, is there?"

He stopped the car. We were on a busy thoroughfare.

"What's the matter? Why did you stop the car?"

"The car just quit." He eyed me suspiciously, and got out.

He draped himself under the hood for quite some time, as cars whizzed past, the people honking and cheering when the saw the just married signs and streamers and old shoes and tin cans. I tried to crouch under the dashboard.

"Well, come on," he said as he dragged our suitcases from the trunk. "We have to go find a telephone and call a cab."

"What! Walk! On the street! With these clothes on!" I glanced at the suitcases in his hands. "And, and carrying suitcases!" I sputtered.

"Do you want to sit here alone, wearing that dress, in this highly decorated car, while I find a phone?"

I clambered out beside him.

"I'm having a problem figuring this out," Bob said seriously, as we walked along.

"What's that?"

"Well, just a few hours ago, I promised to love you for better or for worse." He paused dramatically. "What I would like to know is; is this the, "Better, or the worse?"

There was nothing that I could think of to say. We just walked on. In our wedding clothes. Down the street. Carrying suitcases. While cars drove past and people gawked and laughed and honked and whistled and shouted.

In retrospect now, I think perhaps that was one of the, "better".

Nothing Seems To Help

"Now where did that man go?" Bob asked.

We were at a small, locally owned lumberyard and the owner had directed Bob to a stack of wood siding near the back of the lot. Bob was maneuvering our van back, as close as he could get, to facilitate loading. Now, he looked around bewildered.

"Do you see him, anywhere?" Bob asked, more directly this time.

"What? Huh?" I mumbled, looking up from a book that had me deeply engrossed. I glanced through the windshield. "Nope, he's not here."

Bob looked disgusted. "Well, he certainly did disappear. Check and see how close I am to that stack of siding."

I stuck my head out the passenger side window and almost fainted.

"Stop! Stop! There he is!"

Bob slammed on the breaks and we jolted to a stop.

"Where is he? Who? What's the matter?"

"The man," I answered "The owner. He's right next to the wood. You very nearly smashed him."

"How'd he get there? You said he wasn't around."

"I guess I just didn't notice him, Dear," I replied meekly.

We went back the next day for a second load. I left my book at home.

"Can you keep an eye on that guy, this time?" Bob demanded.

"Yes, Dear."

He began slowly backing to the stack of wood siding. I was hanging halfway out the passenger side window.

"Okay. Keep going. You're doing fine."

"Watch for that guy," Bob shouted.

"He's not in sight. You're safe. You can get closer. I'll tell you when."

"Do you see the man?" Bob growled.

I ducked back inside and grinned menacingly. "No, Dear. The man is not there. I do not see anyone. Otherwise," I added sarcastically, "I really would have said something. You may proceed with equanimity."

"Huh?" Bob replied, or maybe he said, "Bah."

I returned to hanging out the window, carefully watching for our vanishing friend. Suddenly, someone walked out from behind the wood stack. I quick checked. No, it wasn't the owner. I glanced back at the stack of wood.

"Stop!" I yelled. Too late.

A loud thud and then a strange yowling type sound reached us.

I looked at Bob. "I found the man, Dear," I said.

Bob closed his eyes. "Where?"

"He was on top of that stack of wood that you just bumped into."

A few weeks later, Bob had me call the lumberyard to see if they had some certain size boards. They did. They even offered to deliver them to us, no charge. I thought that was awfully nice.

"Hi," I greeted the man that afternoon. "Just take it back there, just past the barn, please. That's the best place."

He drove behind the barn and unloaded the boards.

"You'll have to back out of here," I told him, "but don't worry. I'll direct you."

He looked very, very worried.

We had a really pretty, temporary fence around the field. Five hundred feet of "X" rail; two wood posts in the form of an "X", connected to the next "X" by two long wood rails.

"Oops," I said, as he misread my hand motions and bumped into the fence.

He jumped out of his truck, and we watched helplessly, as each "X" keeled over, pushing the rails into the next "X". It was a slow motion, genuine, domino effect. It seemed to take a long time for all those "X"s to go down. When the momentum reached the corner posts, they just slowly turned the corner and kept going. It was an interesting sight.

I tried to think of something intelligent to say. Total blank.

"Do you want to deliver the next load, or should we pick it up?" I asked.

"I guess it really doesn't matter." He turned and smiled. "I thought it would be different if I delivered it."

"No," I told him. "Nothing seems to help."

He looked a little despondent. I said, helpfully, "There is one bright spot for you though."

"What's that?"

"We won't be ordering any more lumber for at least six months. Maybe things will have changed by then."

He looked hopeful. Of course, things didn't change.

I Was Not At Fault

"Now, Robert, before anyone tells you any different, it wasn't my fault. I didn't make one wrong move or comment. Not one. And if the police come to haul someone away, I didn't do it."

Bob looked just this side of doubtful. He glanced at our three daughters, who were a perfect picture of studied nonchalance.

"The police are coming?"

"Well, no. Well, maybe," I glowered at the girls and shook my finger at them, "well, they might."

Sally had a business appointment in Duluth. Naturally, her sisters wanted to go, too. So did a friend of mine. For soon to be obvious reasons, I'll just refer to her as Mrs. P. You see, she was the corrupting influence on this trip.

The ride to Duluth was cheerful. With five women in one car, all chattering and laughing and singing; happiness and peace and sheer enjoyment are a natural by-product.

When five men ride in one car together, there is an undeniable aura of power emanating right through the metal and impacting anyone within ten feet of the vehicle, whether it's moving or sitting still.

There is a definite difference. Men are way too serious. And boring. Women are much more cheerful. They have a lot more fun, too.

We got to Duluth early and the others decided that we should all do a bit of shopping. No one consulted me. Everyone was having a grand time, except me, which was fine. Some of us were meant to suffer, so that others can enjoy life. It would have helped if they had noticed my martyrdom. But no, they were so self-absorbed in their own pleasures, that they failed to realize my agony, following them from store to store, while they shopped, shopped, shopped. To baldly assert, that I hate to shop, would, perhaps, overstate my feelings. Perhaps.

Mrs. P. found a store that sold special imported stuff. She bought a little bag full of loose tea made up of spices from all over the planet. It had a very distinctive aroma.

Finally, it was time for Sally's appointment and we all trooped off to the very modern office building where she was to meet with her business people. Lots of classy, important looking people walked back and forth in the huge lobby where we waited.

We waited and waited. Then we waited some more. My, but it was taking a long time. I paced the lobby. Sighed heavily. Paced some more.

Leah and Rebekah and Mrs. P. sat, rather impatiently, on the concrete benches. They all sighed heavily.

"I sure wish she'd hurry up," Mrs. P. complained, "I want to get home and brew up some of this great smelling tea."

"Does it smell really good?" Rebekah wanted to know.

Mrs. P. opened the little bag and stuffed her nose inside.

"Ummm," she ummmed, "here, take a whiff," and she held it out to my little daughter.

"Ummm," Rebekah echoed, "it's heavenly."

"Let me see?" Leah said.

She took the bag and inhaled deeply. "Ummm." Then she stuffed her nose back into the bag and ummed some more.

"Here, give it back. I want to smell it again." Rebekah again.

Mrs. P. grabbed the bag. "Hey, it's my tea. The way you guys are going, there won't be any smell left for brewing."

She buried her nose back down into the bag and sniffed noisily.

People began to stare as they walked by.

"Cut it out, you guys," I hissed.

"Here Mom, you should smell this. Boy it smells like Christmas and summertime all rolled into one."

They were all passing the bag back and forth now, giggling, and purposely attracting attention to themselves. Acting very immature.

"Behave yourselves," I said in my most authoritative voice. Trying to be the grownup influence.

Nobody behaved. People began to slow down and stare as they went by.

"You guys are embarrassing me." Big mistake.

They continued this appalling behavior until Sally came out of the office. She, too, buried her nose into the bag and sniffed the tea. "Umm," she said.

By now, I noticed, people were not just staring as they walked by. They were clumping together, whispering and nodding in our direction. I hurriedly ushered everybody out to the car.

The ride home from Duluth was cheerful. With four out of five women in one car chattering and laughing and singing, the natural by-product is happiness, peace and sheer enjoyment.

From now on, I decided, I'll ride with the men.

Credit Where Credit Is Due

I did something right.

Our volunteer fire department's women's auxiliary was having a fundraiser. Sharon and I are firemen in our department; but we are also a part of the auxiliary. We helped, of course, with the spaghetti dinners. We mopped the floors and helped to get all of the tables and chairs set up. The other ladies in the auxiliary were also very busy. They had been shopping and cleaning, and were now getting ready to do the chopping and cooking. The hum of important, busy activity was noticeable all through the fire hall.

"We need those trucks moved out of the way," one of the ladies said. "Is there anyone here who knows how to move them?"

Everyone stopped what they were doing and looked around. Sharon was outside, out of sight, shaking out rugs. That left me. Being an extremely modest person, I didn't want to just shout out about my abilities. Instead, I smiled knowledgeably, pulled myself up to my, very nearly five foot four height and swaggered about in front of everyone.

"Where's Sharon?" someone said, looking over my head. "She's a fireman. I'll bet she can move the trucks."

"I'll get her, "I mumbled, and went, dejectedly, to the door.

"Hey, Sharon! They want you to move the trucks."

"Me?"

"Yeah, you."

"Okay," she said affably, "but I wonder, why me?"

I didn't say anything.

She climbed into the big red truck and started the procedures.

"Where'd the brake go?" she shouted to me.

I climbed up and showed her the brake release. She couldn't get it down. I climbed into the passenger side and closed the door. I released the brake.

"Thanks," she said.

She carefully maneuvered the truck outside and parked. I pulled the brake lever up.

"Do they want me to move that big tanker truck, too?"

I nodded gloomily.

She climbed into the cab of the truck that I secretly refer to as, the monster. She began the procedures.

"Hey, Darlene," she shouted, "where's the starter on this monster?"

Apparently, she felt the same as I about that truck.

I clambered aboard.

"There it is," I told her. "That stick-shift looking thingy. You have to pull it forward. Or is it backward?"

She pulled on the starter. Nothing happened. She pulled again. Still nothing.

"Got any ideas, kid?" she asked.

"Scoot over," I told her.

She scooted. I slipped into the driver's seat. I pulled the starter. Nothing happened. I reached down with both hands and pulled with all my might. The truck roared into life.

"You drive it out of here," Sharon said.

I smiled proudly, put it into gear, eased the truck outside, and parked it.

"Good show, old girl," Sharon said, clapping me on the back. "You did it."

She went back to the shaking out of rugs and I went back into the fire hall where the other women were busy.

"The trucks have been moved," I announced with magnificent, grandiose humility.

The ladies turned and nodded their heads in acknowledgement. They were all very busy.

Soon, another fireman came into the hall. He had come to move the trucks.

"We didn't need you," one of the ladies told him with a laugh. "We have our own fireman right here on the spot. SHE can move the trucks just as good as you men can."

"I can see that. Who moved them?"

I turned and strolled calmly and modestly to the center of the station. My feet barely touching the floor, my head floating in clouds of glory.

"Sharon did," they told him.

The Fine Art of Assertiveness

Way back, when I was a young mommy with young children, I began to read a lot about being assertive. "Do not let others walk all over you." "You are just as important as anyone." "Be assertive." "Stand tall." "Walk tall." And stuff like that there.

A friend of mine was also being bombarded with these self-assertive truths, and we decided that we needed to do just that. Be assertive. It was no great feat to convince our respective husbands that we needed some time away from house and children. They readily agreed that a few hours a week for us to go, "out," was a reasonable suggestion. They would manage the child activities at home.

"Out," to us meant two hours of swimming, and then relaxing over pie and coffee at a different eatery each Tuesday night. We would discuss politics and religion and world news and fashion. Sometimes we would touch on other popular subjects. Like assertiveness.

We agreed that it was essential for a person to stand up for their own rights, and that it was foolish to let someone else control what they, themselves, would do. This was an especially important subject to us, as we both tended to be, "mousy," and often allowed ourselves to be pushed around by others.

One particular evening, after our swimming, we decided to have our pie and coffee at a cute little diner not too far from home. Neither of us had been there before.

Several minutes after we had ensconced ourselves in a booth, the waitress came over to our table. She stood there, order pad and pen in hand. She rested one elbow on her hip and glowered at us.

"You want somethin'?" she snapped.

"Uh, yes," I said matter-of-factly. "What kind of pie do you have?"

"It's on the menu."

"Oh," Cheryl and I replied meekly as we each quickly grabbed a menu and scanned the pie list.

"I'll have strawberry," Cheryl said affably.

"All outta strawberry."

"Then, I'll have pecan pie. You're not out of pecan pie, are you?" Cheryl, being assertive.

My admiration for my friend grew. I wanted to emulate that assertiveness, but I couldn't think of any assertive way to order; so I just said, "I'll have lemon meringue." I knew that they had lemon meringue, because I had seen a slice in their little glass covered pie carousel.

We each ordered a cup of coffee.

Much, much later, our waitress presented our order to us: one slice of pecan pie, one slice of lemon meringue pie, two cups of coffee and a plate of french-fries.

She slapped the order ticket down on the table and stood there, scowling over us. She had her fists on her hips, one elbow pointing north and the other pointing south. Obviously, a fellow believer in assertiveness.

I looked at the plate of unordered french-fries and then looked helplessly at Cheryl. I raised my eyebrows, questioningly. She sucked in her lower lip, smiled a wan smile, and reached for the french-fries.

"Well, shall we have our french-fries first?" She took one and nibbled at it in a friendly way.

"Sure, why not?" I agreed.

The waitress left without saying a word.

We had eaten our way down to the last half-dozen french-fries when Cheryl leaned over and stared into the plate. She looked up at me. Her face was green.

"A cockroach," she whispered, hoarsely, "a french-fried cockroach."

I confirmed this horrifying statement with a long, long look at the plate.

We looked around for the waitress. She was sitting down, reading a book.

"You call her," I said.

"Not me," my friend replied. "You want her, you call her."

We sat there silently for awhile, then I glanced back at the waitress who was now leaning on the counter. She was smiling. It wasn't a friendly smile. Slowly, I covered the offending sight with a napkin.

We ate our pie in silence.

"You know, my friend," I said at last. "I'm thankful for one thing."

"What's that?" she wanted to know.

"I'm thankful that I'm not eating pecan pie."

When we were done, after much deliberation, we decided that we would finally make an assertive stand. We left a very small tip.

Tell-a-Computer

Carefully, I placed Bob's paycheck into the envelope; then slipped a car payment coupon and a savings ticket in with it.

"Now, watch," I explained patiently to Bob, who was rather dubiously absorbing the whole process of using the brand new, innovative, automatic banking machine.

I inserted the little plastic card into the proper slot; then suspiciously glanced around the bank foyer.

"First you make sure that no one is lurking about, then you punch in your secret code." I punched in our secret code. "Three-nine-o-nine," I said importantly.

"Are you sure?" Bob asked. "Besides, if it's so secret, why say it out loud?"

"Look, Dear, there's no one around to hear, and yes, I'm sure, because I have it written down right here." I showed him the inside of my purse.

He didn't look happy. Bob is old fashioned and doesn't take too well to brand new, innovative technology and stuff, like I do.

The automatic banking machine flashed a message and with much ado, I obeyed its various commands, ending by inserting the envelope that contained the paycheck, savings ticket and car payment coupon. We stood silently, watching it disappear.

"Now what?" Bob asked.

"Now I tell it about the savings deposit and the car payment, and it will say, 'thank you', and send out receipts. Simple."

"Simple is fine, but I don't like the idea that this machine has my endorsed paycheck and I don't have a receipt."

"Relax. Watch," I told him again. "See, it wants to know if there are anymore transactions. I just punch this button and…"

Bob watched as I obeyed the machine. Then it flashed the message, "insert envelope." I smiled and searched for the button to tell it that I had already, "inserted envelope," earlier. There was none.

"Now what?" Bob wanted to know as the machine beamed its command accusingly.

"Well, it wants another envelope," I explained, wringing my hands.

The message began to flash off and on, "insert envelope, insert envelope." The lights seemed to be shouting, "insert envelope, you fool!"

"Will you feed that thing," Bob demanded, "before it blows a fuse!"

"I can't," I wailed, "I already put everything into the first envelope."

"Look," I pleaded with the machine, "I already inserted the envelope, before."

It kept flashing its shouts at me.

"Hello, hello, in there," I knocked on the wall.

"Insert envelope," the machine repeated, "insert envelope."

"I already did, 'insert envelope,'" I shouted into its face.

Suddenly the message disappeared and with an ominous whirring sound, the machine rudely, and perhaps with some exasperation, returned my little plastic card. The foyer was very silent for a full minute.

"Where's my paycheck?" Bob asked quietly.

"I don't know."

"Where's the receipt?"

"I don't know."

"Didn't you say that the teller showed you how to work this thing?"

"Well, yes, she did. But she didn't cover this problem." I paused. "There's no one in there, really, is there?"

"It's Saturday."

"Look, Dear," I said ever so sweetly. "Why don't you go to the car and wait for me. Okay? I'll handle this."

Bob looked unconvinced at the wisdom of this, but reluctantly let me push him out the door.

"Now," I told the machine grimly, "you want envelopes. I'll give you envelopes."

I took a piece of paper and wrote, "Help! This machine has eaten my car payment." I signed my name. This note went into an envelope. Another piece of paper, another note, another envelope. "This is an instant replay of the last envelope," I wrote. I pushed all the right buttons, fed the machine its apparently insatiable diet of envelopes and received the receipts. I went out to the car vindicated and flushed with victory.

Monday morning brought the discovery that our checkbook was in dangerous condition. I called the bookkeeping department of our bank, and when the lady answered, I explained in a very businesslike manner who I was. I asked to transfer funds from our savings to our checking account.

There was a gasp on the other end of the line and she called out to her co-workers, "It's that woman. That Mrs. Hodge. The one who wrote all those notes. Now, she wants to transfer from her savings to her checking."

Laughter wafted over the phone lines. Since this is a rather common occurrence for me, I waited patiently for the general hilarity to subside.

Finally, another lady came on the line. "Mrs. Hodge," she said, and identified herself as the person in charge. "We certainly enjoyed your little notes. What a pleasant way to begin a Monday morning."

I thanked her and transacted my business.

The following weekend, there was no problem with the machine, and the next Tuesday the receipts came in the mail. Then I saw, on the bottom of the page that listed the weekend transactions, a note written in little computer lettering.

"So glad you had no trouble this time. Happy to be of service to you."

My very first fan letter.

Something New in the Production Line

The clatter, and clank, and chugging, from the factory machines all around, fascinated me. My first day on my first, honest-to-goodness full time job was starting off very well.

The cookie factory had many phases, and the boss explained that I was to be trained in most of them, so that I could be a sort of troubleshooter, if someone became ill.

"We'll start you here," she said as she lifted a metal box and set it on a tilted stand. I peeked inside. It was layered full of cookies in long neat rows. She grabbed a complete row, her hands about shoulder width apart, held them in the air a second or two, then smoothly tilted her hands and slipped the entire row of cookies into a long narrow, open-faced tube. I called it a half-tube. The half-tube, at measured intervals, dropped the cookies, one at a time, onto a conveyer belt. A hopper measured a dollop of icing and then another half-tube dropped a cookie on top as the conveyer belt moved them on to the packaging section. We were making sandwich cookies.

There were five or six open-faced or half-tubes, for me to keep filled, but the boss cautioned me to start by picking up five cookies at a time, until I learned the right technique.

Well, of course, I'm not entirely stupid. Hadn't I just watched her use the right technique? She stood beside me as I hurriedly placed five cookies into position. Ridiculously easy, I thought. She remained a few minutes more, then went on her way to oversee the rest of the crew.

Ha! She was gone. No more of this, baby-play-five-cookies, for me. I reached into the can and grabbed a whole row. They peaked in the middle and cookies exploded out of that box like shrapnel. They bounced into my face, flew across the conveyer belt, landed on the icing hoppers and fell, naturally, to the floor. I tried frantically to straighten out the mess that I had created and still maintain the tubes, but I couldn't keep up, and suddenly the conveyer stopped. I looked around sheepishly. It seemed very quiet; as though the entire factory had come to a complete halt because of me. I now understood the term, "holding up production." Humbled, I spent the next few hours picking up rows of five. I added a sixth and seventh by coffee break time. By then the sides of my fingers were so sore, I could barely hold a cup.

Lunchtime found me with a band aide on every one of my tender fingertips. Those little cookies were very, very sharp.

"You'll toughen up," the other ladies told me as they admired my bandages.

"I just hope that I can keep improving my technique," I explained. "I'm up to three-fourths of a row now," I added proudly.

"Good," the conveyor operator exclaimed. "We'll speed up the belt now. You should be able to keep up.

I smiled weakly. "Sure," I said.

The rest of the afternoon was a whirling, frantic race against the machines. They had speeded up the conveyor belt to a dizzying motion, and I whipped row upon row of cookies into the half-tubes.

Sometimes cookies would explode into the air, but rushing and heavy mental concentration kept me in good standing. We didn't have to stop production, even once, for me to catch up.

The end of the shift found me dragging up the stairs to the locker room. I was exhausted, yet somehow exhilarated. I had become a full-fledged member of society. A producer of consumer goods, a worker, a taxpayer. I had taken my place beside other working, productive citizens of our great country. I had even sacrificed something of myself. My poor, aching fingertips. I looked proudly at my hands, then caught my breath in horror. The band aids were gone.

Who Moved The Bridge?

It really isn't seemly for grandmas to swagger. So I don't. I mean just because I have a first place trophy, that is, a first place karate trophy, for fighting. That's no reason to brag and stuff like that there. After all, I only had to beat one other old lady, er, I mean, uh, well, anyway she was a little bit younger than I, and she was pretty tough. I only beat her by one point. I don't like to brag and all, but it was first place. The karate trophy, I mean.

Still flush with victory, a year or so later, I decided to enter a sword form competition in a huge national karate tournament down in Minneapolis/St. Paul.

For weeks and weeks and months and months, I trained and practiced and worked my poor, pitiful body until the sword and I were one unit. I was ready. Ready to face the challenge. Ready to do my best. Ready to take my place beside the great swordsmen of the world. The fearsome samurai warriors and Zorro and Captain Bonnie, that lady pirate, that all the other pirates were in awe of, and all those other sword guys.

The exciting day arrived. The judges were ready. I was ready. At last, they called my name. I ran forward, bowed, and began.

The first move, in this particular form, was an awesome move. It had me rising, straight from a kneeling position, holding a full size sword in front of my face with both hands, arms extended. Now, this may not sound like such an awesome move, until you remember that we're talking about a little old grandma, here. I half-expected cheers and flowers and all sorts of accolades to surround me, just for accomplishing that maneuver, alone. Because, you see, I could actually accomplish this without help, without groans and without bones creaking.

I waited for just a few seconds. No cheers, flowers, etc., so, I continued though the rest of the form, ferociously slicing and dicing and kicking and using loud kia's. The loud kia's are for if you don't scare your opponent with the sword, you shatter his confidence with your fearsomeness, and all that. You have to look very ferocious while doing all of this, because, I mean, if you look like your having a good time while slicing and dicing and kicking, well, people may want to check into your mental well-being.

All went beautifully until the next to last move. A slight misstep. I hoped the judges didn't notice. The judges noticed. I took second.

Now, second place at a national karate tournament is pretty good. I accepted the trophy with great humility. It was nearly three feet tall. I shyly carried it around to where Bob was busy judging another group. He beamed approval. With an even greater air of humility, I carried it to show Micah and his friends.

They were impressed. They suggested that I put it in a locker, or some other place of safety, until it was time to leave. I quietly demurred. It wasn't really too heavy, I informed them. I modestly carried it around to show anyone who would admire it. When we finally got home, that weekend, I reluctantly decided that it would probably be in poor taste to carry it into church with me. Ditto the grocery store.

The trophy rested in a place of honor on the kitchen table at our house until, well, until the snickering and obviously, envious remarks by some, forced it into a resting place of honorable retirement. Out if sight.

Several of my grandchildren had been suitably impressed, however, and decided that they wanted to watch me compete in a less distant karate tournament held in Superior, Wisconsin. I was very pleased. With some apprehension, their parents allowed them to travel across the state border, alone with me.

A small disclaimer here, I have to admit that I really didn't practice as much as I should have. Actually, the weeks that led up to this fun weekend had been very hectic. There really hadn't been a lot of time to practice at all. No matter. I was prepared, mentally and physically. My recall of all the separate moves would fall smoothly into place as soon as I began, I knew. As for sparring, who needed to practice? Didn't I have a first place trophy to prove my exceptional, innate ability?

"Now don't be too shocked at your grandma when you see how fierce and powerful she is," I warned the children.

We found the city of Superior right where it belonged, on the other side of that great, big, long bridge across from Duluth. There really seemed no need for the babble of teen voices that apparently marveled to be at our destination with no mishap. I explained to them all, that I had made this trip numerous times and this time I knew how not to get lost. They declared, loyally, that I indeed, seemed to have an undeserved and sullied reputation.

The tournament began. At last, the weapons event. My turn. I ran forward, bowed and began. First move. A slight pause. No accolades here, either. Then, on through the form. My mind seemed one or possibly, two steps behind my body. Halfway through, I deeply regretted my lack of practice. I hoped that the judges wouldn't notice my lack of practice. Apparently, they had noticed. I didn't even place. My own grandchildren had noticed enough to comment negatively.

"Boy, Grandma, you sure didn't look very fierce or powerful, or ferocious. You just looked like a sweet, little old lady out there waving a sword around."

The fighting/sparring didn't go much better. Frankly, I got beat up by a nineteen-year-old kick boxer. I did place, but the trophy was so small it would fit in my jacket pocket. It wasn't hard to accept this tiny, little, itsy, bitsy miniature with great humility. I skulked around for the last few hours of the tournament pretending to be too very, very busy to bother about such frivolities as trophies.

After everyone had climbed back into the car and we began to wend our way home, I explained my folly in taking situations for granted. Even I should have practiced, I admitted, humbly. I smiled sweetly and told them that a true test of maturity was to take whatever happens in stride and not get upset over circumstances. I turned west, and headed back to Minnesota.

The bridge was gone.

"Who moved the bridge?" I gasped. "It was right here when we came over this morning. They've moved it. In just that short of time, some evil person has moved the bridge."

The children were dumbfounded. They had never before experienced a situation like this. They mumbled to one another. I didn't quite hear what it was they were saying.

We searched around the various streets and finally discovered the bridge's, secret, new location. We quickly crossed over before we were caught in some other transfer of, who knew what, proportion.

After delivering the children to their respective parents, I mulled the day over and over in my mind. There was only one obvious conclusion.

As I say, it really isn't seemly for grandmas to swagger. Especially, if there is no substantial reason to swagger. So, for obvious reasons, I don't.

Just Kidding

"What is that?" I gasped.

"It's a baby goat," Bob explained.

"Yes, Dear," I said sweetly, "I can see it's a baby goat. You didn't let me finish the question. What is that doing in my kitchen?"

"Oh," Bob hedged. "Yes, and a very good question, too. You see, Honey," he smiled a big generous smile, "this poor little, motherless goat is afraid to stay in the cold, dark barn with only those big, scary horses."

"Uh huh."

"So he will have to stay in here tonight."

"But I don't WANT a goat in the kitchen."

"Look at his eyes; begging, pleading. How could you throw him out?"

I scowled at Bob, the goat and the kids, (people kind). Everybody was getting into the act.

"All right," I said, "but you guys clean up after it."

"Him," Bob said. "He's a little billy goat."

Later that evening, after barricading the kitchen door, we all went off to our respective beds. All, except little Billy.

"Baa aa aa," he said, trying to climb out of the kitchen to follow us. "Baa aa aa."

"It's amazing, isn't it?" I grumbled, "just how far a little goat can project his little voice."

Bob didn't answer. He figured that the better part of valor is sometimes not only to retreat but also to be quiet.

"Baa aa aa."

Around eleven o'clock I noticed a long quiet spell. At last, I could go to sleep. I wondered, vaguely, why he wasn't calling. My eyes flew open. Maybe he had gotten out of the kitchen and was, even now, eating the curtains in the living room. I switched on the light.

"Baa aa aa," he was still in the kitchen. Outsmarted by a baby goat.

Another thirty minutes of constant calling, finally, thankfully, he quieted down again. I left the light off. He wasn't going to trick me twice.

"Did that little billy finally go to sleep?" Bob whispered.

"Yes," I whispered back, "And it's almost midnight."

"Baa aa aa."

"He's got good ears, too," I snarled and pulled the blanket over my head.

Goats are cute little creatures. They say "baa aa aa," a lot. Their little feet clatter along kitchen floors and they slip and fall, with all four legs splayed out in all four directions. "Baa aa aa," they say. Outside, they run and kick up their heels and eat seedlings trees, and pansies, and peony bushes. I have never caught one eating weeds.

Little Billy grew to be a humungous, over a hundred and fifty pound, Houdini type, he-goat. He learned to lift the latches on all the gates. We tied the gates with ropes. He ate the ropes. We tied the gates with wire. He untwisted the wire. We tied the gates with chains. That wasn't even a challenge, he just worked them loose. He was the hero of the barnyard.

Whenever something would frighten the baby goats, they would run and stand under Billy, and he would arch his neck, and lower his horns, and all manner of creatures would back away. He was a majestic animal.

Billy had just one fault and that was a horrible fault. He loved to be petted. He would lean against people and do a terrific imitation of a cat, he very nearly purred.

Having a friendly billy goat is nice, but they do not smell very nice. In point of fact, they smell awful.

The first reaction that most people have when they get a whiff of these loveable creatures, is to look around wildly, take a deep gasp for fresh air, and reel under the impact of inhaling the noxious fumes that are permeating the air around them. Then their eyes begin to water, their noses flap shut and their faces turn blue.

"Oh, what a pretty pastoral scene," my city friend sighed.

The horses and cows were grazing contentedly. The chickens were scurrying around. The goats were lying, bunched together, watching us.

"Yes, it is pretty," I said.

"But why," her voice sounded sad, "why do you have that one, poor goat tied up, away over there, by itself?"

"Oh," I told her by way of explanation, "that's Billy."

"But why is he tied?"

"Well, uh, he gets out of the fence all of the time, and he eats the flowers and such."

"But why tie him? That seems so cruel. Is he mean? Don't you care for him?"

"Yes, we care for him and no, he's not mean. Actually, he's quite loveable."

She walked over to where Billy stood at the end of his chain. "Poor Billy," she said soothingly. "Are they mistreating you?" She reached out her hand to pet him.

I held my breath.

Civilized Duty

"Bob," I said to my unsuspecting husband, "I have something Very Important to talk to you about."

"Something very important?" he questioned.

"No, Dear, not 'very important', lower case, something Very Important."

"Oh," he said, "I see. Very Important."

He sat down and pulled a chair opposite to him. He waited.

"Do you remember," I began slowly, "back when I was handling the budget and we were always getting those unkind little letters and phone calls about payments and stuff?"

He shuddered and nodded his head, eyeing me suspiciously.

"Well, I've been thinking about it, and I believe that with my former experience in the field of budgeting, well, Honey, it's my duty as a citizen, to run for political office."

"What experience? You never could balance the checkbook, let alone the budget."

"My point exactly. See, I would fit right in with what's happening now. I probably couldn't balance the government's budget either, but voters would feel more confident, knowing that I was there, and that I was really trying and that I didn't make any rash promises."

"You've thought this out, have you?"

"Yes, I even have a platform."

Bob sighed, "so tell me."

"No special favors to interest groups. Anybody wants money from the government, just come to me and I'll give it to them. Anybody," I smiled at Bob's shocked look.

"The kicker is," I said, "that the money that they get for their special interest will be taxed. One hundred fifty-five percent. That way, the government can make some profit, for a change."

"But, Honey, no one would want to get money that would be taxed like that."

"That's right. See, we would be saving globs of dollars or making globs of dollars. I think that's pretty clever of me."

"Yes," he said, "it is clever."

"No gun control, either."

"That's good," Bob smiled.

"Guns don't kill people," I explained, "cars do."

"What?"

"Sure. Cars kill people. So, I would make a law. Only one car per household. Families would have to be together more. So, that strengthens the home. The one car law saves on pollution, too. And, don't worry about those car makers and mechanics and sales people being put out of work. Only cars that are three years old and newer would be allowed on the highways. And, they would have to be totally overhauled, annually. That will generate more jobs, and competition for all this work and will bring the prices down."

"So, a vote for you, is a vote for car control."

"Sounds good, doesn't it?"

"I can hardly wait to write your name on the ballot."

"Thank you, Dear, and there is no scandal associated with me, either. I've never cheated on my taxes, pilfered money, had an affair, belonged to a subversive organization. I've never gone swimming in the nude, I don't reveal other people's deep, dark problems and I never saw a UFO or a rabid rabbit. I'm clean. I'm perfect for the job."

"That's true, but it will take a lot of money for a campaign," Bob said, rather reasonably.

"Right, but I have a plan that I stole from some other guy, somewhere, that I read about."

"That plan being?"

"If everyone who votes for me will give me a dollar, I guarantee that I will only stay in office for a specified time."

"How long?"

"Well, uh, I don't know for sure. It depends on how well I like the job."

"Uh oh, sounds ominous. You're sure that you want to do this?"

"Yep, I have lots of plans and ideas to make our society good again. No more wrestling. No more Country Western music. No more…"

"Hold it. Hold it. What do you mean, 'no more wrestling and Country Western music'?"

"Now don't get upset, Bob. I know that you and some of our best friends like Country Western music and we even have people in the family who like wrestling. But, well, in this business you just can't let friendship influence your decisions. I want our country to be cultured and civilized."

"Honey," Bob said rather carefully, "I'm afraid that some people will disagree with your idea of culture. Perhaps they may even enjoy being uncivilized."

He smiled gently at my disappointment.

"Tell you what. If I take you to see that Evander Holyfield-Buster Douglas fight on the big screen in Tower, will that help you feel better? And forget your political ambitions?"

"You'll take me to see the big fight? Even though you don't care for boxing? Oh, Bob, you're terrific. Yes! Yes! Yes! Besides, the people probably wouldn't vote for me anyway. They just don't, er, don't…," I struggled for the right words.

"They don't deserve someone as cultured as you," Bob said, quite seriously.

"Right," I agreed.

The Big Fight in Tower

"Back" I snarled, knife poised to defend myself. "Back you beastie."

People at the other tables turned to stare.

"Just give it here," Bob sighed, "I'll eat it."

Obediently, I handed my plate, with the still breathing, fighting bovine barely under control, to Bob. He, being tough and macho and all that sort of stuff, stabbed it with his table utensil, and dragged it onto his plate; thereby restraining it long enough to be devoured.

I ate the potatoes. It really didn't matter. I was too excited to eat a full steak dinner. It was the night of the big Heavyweight Championship Boxing match and we were at the casino in Tower, getting ready to watch the closed circuit showing on the big screen.

"Are you having a good time?" I asked Bob anxiously as we settled into our seats, downstairs.

"I'm having a good time, because I'm with you and you are having a good time," he said.

He's so romantic.

I was determined that the company I kept would not infringe on the night's enjoyment.

John, Paulette's husband, hates boxing.

Bob, my husband, tolerates boxing, sort of, but hates spending money; especially on something so frivolous as mere entertainment.

Paulette, who enjoys boxing as much as I do, had been contradicting me all evening.

"Why are you wearing a skirt to a boxing match?" she queried when they first arrived at our house.

"The legs of my blue jeans are too tight to wear over my boot tops. I won't wear them tucked inside, and I'm sure not about to wear tennis shoes to a bingo place," I explained, reasonably.

"Why?"

"Because, Paulette, everyone knows that little old ladies in tennis shoes frequent bingo halls. I don't want some guy walking up to us and mistaking us for the aforesaid L.O.L.'s because of your grey hair, and both of us wearing tennis shoes. What if someone came up to us and said, 'Sorry ladies, no bingo tonight'? I'd be highly offended."

"Don't be ridiculous. Nobody would say that. Besides, if anybody's grey hair causes trouble, it'll be yours. You have more than I do."

"Mine is platinum blonde," I retorted loftily.

In the big screen room, nee, bingo hall, we watched a fifteen-minute segment of pre-fight hype. It was exciting. Then, we watched a fifteen-minute segment of pre-fight hype. It was interesting. Then, we watched a fifteen-minute segment of pre-fight hype…, we watched a fifteen-minute segment of pre-fight hype…, we watched… By now, everyone in the room could lip-synch the fifteen-minute segment of pre-fight hype.

"The real stuff should be beginning any minute now," I heard Paulette tell John, soothingly.

"Lord, I hope so," he moaned, his head buried in his hands. "I think I've aged ten years already."

Paulette and I decided to walk around for awhile. We went out into the lobby. We watched people. We watched people walking and talking, putting money into machines. We watched people mutter, get mad, happy, frustrated. Lots of excitement. Lots of noise. We started back into the main room, where the big screen awaited. A young, good-looking guard came up to us. He stood in our path. He glanced at Paulette. He looked down at her feet.

"Sorry ladies," he said gently, "No bingo tonight."

Paulette became incoherent. She staggered backward. I had, very nearly, to help her back to her seat.

"Why did he say that? It was word for word what you said." She glanced apprehensively at me.

"You're spooky," she said, grimly. "Some day, they're going to burn you at the stake."

"It's the tennis shoes," I countered. "Tennis shoes and grey hair do it every time."

I settled her down just as the main event was about to start.

"Look," Bob said, with some astonishment. "There's some people we know."

"Where?" I said, studying the screen carefully.

Bob grabbed my head and twisted it to face the door. "There. Look. I thought that they were going to watch the fight at home."

We signaled our friends over to us. Because of some miscalculations on someone's part, they were unable to watch the fight via their satellite dish, and had to rush, nearly fifty miles, to get to the showing on time. They had just arrived in Tower and Evander Holyfield was just entering the ring.

Shouts and cheers and whistles filled the room, as the boxer climbed purposefully through the ropes. A few deluded souls boo'd. I eyed them darkly, making note of their location. I, however, applauded politely when Buster Douglas came into view.

The fight was on. Round one. Holyfield. Round two. Holyfield. Round three. The deadly right! Knockout! Holyfield! The new champ!

Lots and lots of shouts and cheers and whistles and jumping around. Excitement everywhere. It was terrific.

"Did you have a good time?" I asked Bob anxiously on the way home.

"Great!" he said.

"You liked the fight? You really enjoyed it? You're glad you went?"

"I liked the idea," he said gleefully, "that I paid fifteen dollars a ticket for the steak dinner and four hours of entertainment." He looked at me and grinned. "All that those people who came in late got, was a seven minute fight for the same price. They had to pay two dollars a minute. I got a bargain."

"But mostly you're happy because I'm happy. Right?"

"Huh?" he said. "Oh, right." He smiled a great big, happy smile.

He's so romantic.

About the Author

Hodge began her professional writing career with her very first submission to a nation wide magazine, Home Life. She has since had her own humor column in the Hibbing Daily Tribune for over eight years. She has read many of these columns on Minnesota Public Radio and has been the featured speaker at various civic organizations.

Hodge has also been a freelance reporter for different newspapers, including close-up coverage of the colorful Minnesota governor, Jesse Ventura.

71569120R00137

Made in the USA
Columbia, SC
31 May 2017